"I always look forward to the next publication of Paul Dekar's work. It always contains excellent scholarship while still being written with a great deal of heart. This new book by Dekar does not disappoint. Paul has found a new path on which to discuss why it is Merton continues to matter as we address the big issues of our day."

—**William Apel**, emeritus professor, Linfield University

Thomas Merton

Thomas Merton:
God's Messenger on the Road towards a New World

Paul R. Dekar

FOREWORD BY
Christine M. Bochen

AFTERWORD BY
Mark C. Meade

CASCADE *Books* · Eugene, Oregon

THOMAS MERTON: GOD'S MESSENGER ON THE ROAD TOWARDS
A NEW WORLD

Cascade Books
An Imprint of Wipf and Stock Publishers
199 W. 8th Ave., Suite 3
Eugene, OR 97401

www.wipfandstock.com

PAPERBACK ISBN: 978-1-5326-7083-1
HARDCOVER ISBN: 978-1-5326-7084-8
EBOOK ISBN: 978-1-5326-7085-5

Cataloguing-in-Publication data:

Names: Dekar, Paul R., author. | Bochen, Christine M., foreword. | Meade, Mark
C., afterword.

Title: Thomas Merton : God's messenger on the road towards a new world /
by Paul R. Dekar ; foreword by Christine M. Bochen ; afterword by Mark C.
Meade.

Description: Eugene, OR : Cascade Books, 2021 | Includes bibliographical refer-
ences.

Identifiers: ISBN 978-1-5326-7083-1 (paperback) | ISBN 978-1-5326-7084-8
(hardcover) | ISBN 978-1-5326-7085-5 (ebook)

Subjects: LCSH: Merton, Thomas, 1915–1968.

Classification: BX4705.M542 D45 2021 (print) | BX4705.M542 D45 (ebook)

05/28/21

I dedicate this book to Nancy Rose Dekar. My best friend and partner for over fifty years, Nancy consistently encourages and inspires me. In her daily life, Nancy does justice, is compassionate, and is humble. I am grateful for her love.

Contents

Foreword

READING THIS BOOK IN spring 2020, in the midst of a global pandemic and worldwide calls for social justice in the wake of the murder of George Floyd, I could not help thinking of "Earthquake," one of the "Freedom Songs" Thomas Merton wrote in 1964 for young African American tenor Robert Lawrence Williams. Inspired by Isaiah 52, the song proclaims that "the old world is gone" and "a new world is born"—a world without hate and oppression, a world without war, a world of peace and justice. The song's refrain resonates with the deep hunger for justice and demands for change that resound around the world today.

> So tell the earth to shake
> With marching feet
> Of messengers of peace
> Proclaim my law of love
> To every nation
> Every race.

Thomas Merton was himself such a messenger of peace, a herald of "a new world" being born. Indeed, Merton was, as Robert Lawrence Williams would tell him, "God's messenger." In choosing this appellation as the title of his book, Paul Dekar opted for an image that speaks to vocation—Merton's and ours. Merton was a person of faith who chose to live a life of silence and solitude as a Trappist monk, but that was not all there was to his vocation. As he wrote in a letter to friends: "There are three gifts I have received, for which I can never be grateful enough: first, my Catholic faith; second, my monastic vocation; third, the calling to be a writer and share my beliefs with others."[1]

---

1. Merton, *Thomas Merton: A Life in Letters*, 7.

Thus, thrice blessed, Merton the contemplative spoke out, through his life and writings, *against* war and violence in all its forms and *for* nonviolence and peace. In *Thomas Merton, God's Messenger on the Road to a New World*, Paul Dekar invites readers to reflect on the wisdom, practice, and vision that Merton left behind as signposts for our journeys into a new world.

Attentive to God's voice speaking in the silence of his heart, Merton also heard the cries of human suffering in the "body of broken bones" that is humanity.

> All over the face of the earth the avarice and the lust of men breed divisions among them, and the wounds that tear men from union with one another widen and open out into huge wars. Murder, massacres, revolution, hatred, the slaughter and torture of the bodies and souls of men, the destruction of cities by fire, the starvation of millions, the annihilation of populations, and finally the cosmic inhumanity of atomic war: Christ is massacred in His members, torn limb from limb. God is murdered in men.[2]

Yet through his contemplative practice, Merton was able to look beyond the illusions and fictions that distort our sense of ourselves and others and divide us from one another to the truth of our common humanity—a unity grounded in our creation in the image of God. This vision of the human and of humanity itself crystalized in his now-famous epiphany at Fourth and Walnut and, with that awakening, came an expanded sense of his monastic vocation that brought with it a calling to speak out with courage of a prophet against injustice.

> I was suddenly overwhelmed with the realization that I loved all these people, that they were mine and I theirs, that we could not be alien to one another even though we were total strangers. It was like waking from a dream of separateness . . . I have the immense joy of being *man*, a member of the human race in which God Himself became incarnate . . . it was as if I suddenly saw the secret beauty of their hearts . . . the core of their reality, the person that each one is in God's eyes.[3]

Seeing humans—himself included—in this light, a divine light, amplified his sense of responsibility. "My solitude . . . is not my own," Merton concluded.

---

2. Merton, *New Seeds of Contemplation*, 71.
3. Merton, *Conjectures of a Guilty Bystander*, 156–58, Merton's emphasis.

The journal entry in which Merton recorded his experience in Louis-ville includes another epiphanic encounter—one less well-known but no less significant. It was sparked by the "fabulous pictures" in *The Family of Man*, a collection of photographs presented in an exhibit curated by Edward Steichen at New York's Museum of Modern Art. What Merton saw in the book was nothing less than "a picture of Christ." He writes, "There, there is Christ in my own Kind, my own Kind—'Kind' which means 'likeness' and which means 'love' and which means 'child' . . . there is only the great secret between us that we are all one Kind."[4] The insight of unity engendered by these photographs of people living all over the world—people of all ages, skin colors, and cultures as well as the sight of the people he saw in Louisville strengthened Merton's belief that, indeed, we are all part of the human family.

This "great secret" of our essential unity is at the core of his message for those of us who, as Paul Dekar suggests in the title of this book, strive to make our way towards a new world. Surely, we are, as Merton said, just before his death, "already one." Yet there is much work to be done. In the essays collected in this book, Dekar shows how Merton engaged the work, wrestling with obstacles to unity and illuminating a pathway forward.

Paul Dekar takes inspiration from the prophet Micah, who spells out what God requires of those who seek to follow God: "to act justly and to love kindness and to walk humbly with your God" (Mic 6:8). The prophet's directives provide the organizational framework for the book's first three sections: "Doing Justice," "Loving Kindness," and "Walking Humbly." These serve as the foundation for the fourth section, "Merton's Embrace of the Other." In the chapters that comprise each of these sections, Dekar invites readers to delve into a host of issues that concerned Merton—tech-nology, violence and war, racial injustice, ecological destruction—issues that Merton addressed in light of his faith, contemplative prayer, and un-wavering conviction about the fundamental unity of the human family that can heal the breach that divides people.

The breach is real and the demand for "Doing Justice" is a matter of life and death. With words that could as easily been written today, Merton cut to the heart of the matter: "we have created for ourselves a culture which is not yet livable for mankind as a whole."[5] Dekar reminds us that Merton saw injustice at the heart of "all contemporary American problems: race, war . . .the flight from reality into myth and fanaticism, the growing brutality and irrationality of American mores."[6]

4. Merton, *Search for Solitude*, 183.

5. Merton, *Conjectures of a Guilty Bystander*, 73.

6. Merton, *Conjectures of a Guilty Bystander*, 76.

Dekar focuses on two issues of serious concern in our world today. In "Technology and the Loss of Paradise," he explores Merton's critique of technology and the abuses that stem from its unmindful and irresponsible use and the ecological devastation that is the byproduct of such misuse. In "Thomas Merton on Racial Justice," Dekar illuminates Merton's thinking on the realities of racial injustice in the mid 1960s through an examination of his correspondence with friends and allies—Fr. August Thompson, Robert Lawrence Williams, and James Baldwin—and a discussion of Merton's essays on the race question. Merton's starkly realistic reading of the plight of the black person in America is tempered by a hopefulness rooted in faith. Underlying the social issues which Dekar touches upon here, including violence and war and ecological imbalance, is, according to Merton, a spiritual crisis.

"Doing Justice" demands "Loving Kindness." In this section of the book, we are faced with an urgent question: what does it mean to live as a member of the human race? On this point, Merton's response, expressed in the example of his life, is as eloquent as are his writings. As Dekar reminds us, Merton found himself in the new desert of compassion where the measure is mercy. Cultivation of kindness, compassion, and mercy calls for metanoia, for ongoing conversion. The two chapters—"The Wilderness of Compassion" and "Ishi: Messenger of Hope"—illustrate the power of compassion and the pain experienced in its absence.

"Loving Kindness" necessitates "Walking Humbly." Thus, Dekar turns our attention to cultivating the practices of silence, solitude, and stillness. With Merton as our guide, Dekar invites readers to reflect on what walking humbly with God entails. Humility, as Merton came to know, "consists in being precisely the person you actually are before God."[7] In the three chapters of this section, Dekar delves into the contemplative roots of Merton's commitment to justice. In "The Power of Silence" and "Silence as Attention and Antidote," Dekar illuminates the centrality of silence in Merton's contemplative practice. In "Divinization in Merton," Dekar introduces us to what we might term Merton 's anthropology.

The practices of doing justice, loving kindness, and walking humbly with God culminate in what Dekar terms "Merton's Embrace of the Other." Justice, kindness, humility—as Dekar skillfully demonstrates—are powerful antidotes to "forces that foster suffering, like consumerism, militarism, environmental decline, individualism and the collapse of community." Imagining Merton in dialogue with Thich Nhat Hanh and Martin Luther King Jr., reflecting on what Merton learned about nonviolence from Gandhi and about indigenous peoples from his former novice Ernesto Cardenal, Dekar

---

7. Merton, *New Seeds of Contemplation*, 99.

invites us to unpack what he calls "theology of embrace." It is a theology that calls for a "shift from confrontation and violence to dialogue and embrace." Dekar demonstrates how the pathway delineated by Micah's teaching leads to an ever more inclusive vision of the human family and an openness to the world's religious traditions.

We owe Paul Dekar a word of gratitude for the insightful ways in which he illuminates the meaning and relevancy of Merton's wisdom and witness. Written over a span to time and for a variety of audiences, these chapters will appeal to a wide range of readers—those already familiar with Merton and those just discovering him. For the former, this book is an opportunity to consider and reconsider central themes of Merton's legacy in the light of Dekar's fresh insights. For the latter, the book is an invitation to dig more deeply into Merton's own writings on topics of particular interest.

I believe readers will appreciate, as I do, Paul Dekar's approach to Merton, which combines the insight, care, and curiosity of an accomplished scholar with the passionate energy and vision of a spiritual seeker and peace activist. I remember something Merton wrote to young Jim Forest: "In the end . . . it is the reality of personal relationship that saves everything." Certainly, this was true for Merton who knew well the joy and sustaining energy of friendship, the wisdom shared by teachers and mentors, the inspiration and example of spiritual guides, the strength drawn from belonging to a community, the courage to be gained by sharing in a common struggle for justice. As he illuminates Merton's message for us, Paul Dekar affords readers a glimpse of his own experience of "the reality of personal relationship that saves everything." By sharing his own stories of encounters with teachers, mentors, friends, spiritual guides, fellow seekers, and above all with Thomas Merton—as persons who illuminated and continue to illuminate his own road to a new world, Paul Dekar invites his readers to the same. It is not enough to read more about Merton nor even to read Merton; we need to open ourselves to encountering his witness and wisdom on personal terms, allowing ourselves to be challenged and transformed, as together we move along to the road toward a new world.

—Christine M. Bochen

Professor Emerita of Religious Studies, Nazareth College

Acknowledgments

Chapter One: "Technology and the Loss of Paradise." In *Thomas Merton, Monk on the Edge*, edited by Ross Labrie and Angus Stuart, 65–78. North Vancouver: Thomas Merton Society of Canada, 2012.

Chapter Two: "Thomas Merton on Racial Justice." *Merton Annual* 32 (2019) 137–54.

Chapter Three: "Wilderness of Compassion," *Merton Seasonal* 45, 2 (2020) 20–24.

Chapter Four: "Ishi: Messenger of Hope." In *We Are Already One: Thomas Merton's Message of Hope; Reflections to Honor His Centenary (1915–2015)*, edited by Gray Henry and Jonathan Montaldo, 232–34. Louisville: Fons Vitae, 2014.

Chapter Five: "The Power of Silence." *Fellowship* 69 (2003) 15–16.

Chapter Six: "Silence as Attention and Antidote." *Merton Seasonal* 40.1 (2015) 16–19.

Chapter Seven: "Divinization in Merton." Paper read at the 13th ITMS general meeting.

Chapter Eight: "Thich Nhat Hanh, Martin Luther King, Jr., and Thomas Merton on Retreat." *Weavings* 30.1 (2014) 10–15.

Chapter Nine: "Thomas Merton on Gandhi." In *Merton and Hinduism*, edited by David Odorisio, forthcoming. Louisville: Fons Vitae, 2021.

Chapter Ten: "Thomas Merton's Embrace of "The Other." In "Letters with Ernesto Cardinal." Paper proposed for the 17th ITMS general meeting.

Review of *Returning to Reality: Thomas Merton's Wisdom for a Technological World*, by Phillip M. Thompson. *Merton Seasonal* 38 (Spring 2013) 39–40.

Review of *Pursuing the Spiritual Roots of Protest: Merton, Berrigan, Yoder, and Muste at the Gethsemani Abbey Peacemakers Retreat*, by Gordon Oyer. *Merton Annual* 28 (2015) 215–38.

Review of *Interreligious Dialogue: An Anthology of Voices Bridging Cultural and Religious Divides*, edited by Christoffer H. Grundmann. *Missiology* 46.4 (2018) 430–31.

Review of *A Poor and Merciful Church: The Illuminative Ecclesiology of Pope Francis*, by Stan Chu Ilo. *Missiology*, forthcoming.

Review of *The Martyrdom of Thomas Merton: An Investigation*, by Hugh Turley and David Martin. *Merton Seasonal* 43.4 (Winter 2018) 37–39.

Review of *Superabundantly Alive: Thomas Merton's Dance with the Feminine*, by Susan McCaslin and J. S. Porter. *Hamilton Arts and Literature*, December 17, 2018.

I am grateful to the editors of previously published material for permission to revise and include the articles in this book.

Introduction: Why Merton Matters

He has told you, O mortal, what is good;

and what does the Lord require of you

but to act justly and to love kindness

and to walk humbly with your God.

—Micah 6:8 (NRSV)

ANOTHER BOOK ON THOMAS Merton? Absolutely! More than any other North American writing between the Second World War and 1968, when he died, Merton called people to act justly, love kindness, and walk humbly. By his critique of technology, a major impediment for people to follow Jesus; by his writing on contemplative prayer; by his interfaith outreach, and through his witness against racism, war, and degradation of nature, Merton still matters.

In a June 2010 interview, Martin E. Marty, Fairfax M. Cone Distinguished Service Professor of the History of Modern Christianity at the University of Chicago, senior *Christian Century* editor, Lutheran pastor, and co-supervisor of my doctoral work responded to a question about the view of some in the church, even senior leaders, who thought Merton was passé, problematic, and should be ignored. Marty replied, "Come back in twenty years and see who is remembered! Of course, this is the ying/yang, there will always be conflicting interpretations, but a *dismissal* of him [Merton] would be absurd."[1]

On September 24, 2015, in a speech before a joint session of the US Congress, Pope Francis cited Merton along with Dorothy Day of the Catholic Worker movement, President John F. Kennedy, and Dr. Martin Luther

---

1. Marty, "Interview about Thomas Merton," 29, Marty's emphasis.

King Jr., as notable Americans who have inspired and continue to inform the path of dialogue needed to resolve the myriad tensions and conflicts of our day. Concerning Merton, the pope said,

> A century ago, at the beginning of the Great War, which Pope Benedict XV termed a "pointless slaughter," another notable American was born: the Cistercian monk Thomas Merton. He remains a source of spiritual inspiration and a guide for many people. In his autobiography he wrote: "I came into the world. Free by nature, in the image of God, I was nevertheless the prisoner of my own violence and my own selfishness, in the image of the world into which I was born. That world was the picture of Hell, full of men like myself, loving God, and yet hating Him; born to love Him, living instead in fear of hopeless self-contradictory hungers." Merton was above all a man of prayer, a thinker who challenged the certitudes of his time and opened new horizons for souls and for the Church. He was also a man of dialogue, a promoter of peace between peoples and religions.[2]

The context of the speech was crucial for two reasons. One was Pope Francis's understanding of leadership. At a time of deep fissures in the United States, he spoke to its political leaders of their duty to recognize and help overcome their differences and walk a path of dialogue.

As well, Pope Francis highlighted Merton as a notable American along with a lay Catholic, a former president, and a Protestant minister. The pope did not hail anyone else associated with the Roman Catholic Church. By contrast, ten years earlier, the editors of the first Catholic catechism for adults in the United States excluded Merton despite the fact that an earlier draft highlighted the story of his conversion. By omitting Merton, the editors acceded to the view of some Merton critics that he was not sufficiently Catholic.[3]

Merton still matters not simply as a quintessential Catholic but also as one who called people to work to heal divisions in the United States and worldwide. In Merton's lifetime, the so-called Cold War divided the United States and its allies from the former Soviet Union and its allies. While movements for civil rights, gay rights, and women's liberation gained traction, with some victories, they also fueled divisions, wounds too deep to be healed by legislation or courts of law. Nevertheless, Merton remained

---

2. Francis, "Transcript: Pope Francis's Speech to Congress," para. 27. The pope quoted the first paragraph of the North American edition of *The Seven Storey Mountain*, published in Britain as *Elected Silence*.

3. Berger, "What Pope Francis Can Teach."

steadfast in his support for Dr. Martin Luther King Jr., and others promoting freedom, justice, love, and truth.

On the last day of January 2015, the centenary of Merton's birth, *The Merton Seasonal* published a number of essays on *Why Merton Still Matters*. The editor Pat O'Connell observed, "Perhaps Gosia Poks sums up best what all the essays are saying in one way or another: 'Ultimately, Merton matters because he shows that the Sermon on the Mount still matters.'"[4]

As a monk from 1941 to 1968 in the traditions of Western Christian monasticism, Merton committed to live in poverty, chastity, obedience, and stability. He followed *The Rule of Saint Benedict*, a document that has proved a durable guide for monastics in the west since the sixth century.

Benedict was a monk in Norcia, traditionally known in English by the Latin name of Nursia in Umbria, a province in central Italy. Benedict wrote *The Rule* at a time when the monastic ideal had come under threat. Western society crumbled in the face of invasion by so-called barbarians. *The Rule* provided stability and enabled monasteries to sustain people through good as well as dark times. Crucial to its success, Merton regarded Benedictine life as "perfectly simple—the Gospel pure and simple—it liberates us from ourselves by enabling us to give ourselves entirely to God."[5]

Until a schism in 1054, Orthodox and Catholic Christian monastics adhered to common practices. After the break of communion, monks in the East and in the West developed some differences while sharing values common to most religious, ethical, and spiritual traditions.[6] In 1098, Benedictine monks founded the Cistercian order that includes Merton's monastery, the Abbey of Our Lady of Gethsemani.

My journey in reading Merton and other monastic writers began at the University of California at Berkeley where I studied between 1961 and 1965. Living through one of those rare periods in which people made a difference, I participated in civil rights, feminist, anti-Vietnam War, anti-nuclear, and Free Speech protests. Did we believe we could change the world and promote the common good? Many did. Were we also worried that the economic life of the United States with its production of weapons and other technologies of mass destruction endangered human survival? Many did. Did we see that our comfortable lifestyles had made it easy for many people

4. O'Connell, "Editor's Preface," 2.

5. Merton, *Entering the Silence*, 145, entry for December 14, 1947. Merton's *The Waters of Siloe* provides a history.

6. For an introduction to the order, see Aprile, *Abbey of Gethsemani*. Merton's *The Waters of Siloe* also introduces the way of life of a Cistercian monk. Gethsemani retreatants who have visited since Vatican II will find Merton's description of his life during his first decade as a monk as considerably more austere.

to ignore or to be passive regarding the military-industrial complex? Many did. Did people anticipate the consequences of such developments? Many did. Did we agree with prophetic figures like Martin Luther King Jr., who warned of the breakdown of community, erosion of civic consciousness, and immorality of modern war? Many did.

My academic advisor at Berkeley was Eugene Burdick, coauthor of *The Ugly American*, a book that depicts the failures of the US diplomacy in Southeast Asia. Reading the book, and viewing the 1963 film adaptation starring Marlon Brando, influenced me at a very immediate and personal level. Increasingly aware that US involvement in Southeast Asia was misguided, I questioned how to protest. By legal means? By civil disobedience? If the latter, might an arrest threaten my professional goal at the time, to become a lawyer or diplomat?

I joined demonstrations against bomb shelters during which I was handed copies of *The Catholic Worker* with articles by Thomas Merton. The October 1961 issue had an article entitled "The Root of War Is Fear." The November 1961 issue had an article entitled "The Shelter Ethic." These encouraged me to read Merton further.

During my Berkeley years, I frequented City Lights, a literary meeting place and publishing hub founded in 1953 near San Francisco's North Beach and Chinatown districts. The bookstore was a gathering place for Jack Kerouac, Allen Ginsberg, and William Burroughs, writers identified as the "Beat" generation. I bought Merton titles—*Gandhi on Non-Violence, Original Child Bomb*, and *Faith and Violence. Christian Teaching and Christian Practice*—and a collection of poems by the Lawrence Ferlinghetti, who sent books to Merton on May 15, 1968.[7]

The student uprising at Berkeley introduced me to several figures crucial in Merton's story such as Mark van Doran, Gandhi, Nhat Hahn and Martin Luther King Jr. As well, I was reading, discussing, and looking for ways to promote social justice, the common good, and responsible use of technology in pursuit of human freedom and dignity. Especially significant was my involvement during the summer of 1964 in a community development and voter registration organization associated with Saul Alinsky (1909–1972). His *Rules for Radicals* inspired me to dream a new world:

> The great American dream that reached out to the stars has been lost to the stripes. We have forgotten where we came from, we don't know where we are, and we fear where we may be going. Afraid, we turn from the glorious adventure of the pursuit of

---

7. Merton, *Other Side of the Mountain*, 101, entry for May 16, 1968. Merton visited the bookstore on May 15, 1968 (Mott, *Seven Mountains of Thomas Merton*, 523).

happiness to a pursuit of an illusionary security in an ordered, stratified, striped society. Our way of life is symbolized to the world by the stripes of military force. At home we have made a mockery of being our brother's keeper by being his jail keeper. When Americans can no longer see the stars, the times are tragic. We must believe that it is the darkness before the dawn of a beautiful new world; we will see it when we believe it.[8]

Gradually, I came to accept active nonviolence as a and perhaps the only legitimate way to establish God's peace in a world of violence, I joined protests against US military intervention in Southeast Asia. Questioning my career objective, law or diplomacy, I opted to attend Colgate Rochester Divinity College for a trial year.

Throughout my studies, I had a deferment from military service. At seminary, courses in the Bible, history, and ethics confirmed my growing pacifist views. On April 4, 1967, Dr. King spoke at the Riverside Church in New York and urged ministers to give up ministerial immunity and to do alternative service as conscientious objectors. After I read Dr. King's speech, and with needed support from my future wife Nancy, I gave up my seminary exemption, went before my draft board to register as a conscientious objector, and offered to do alternative service. In my application, I cited passages in the Bible as well as such contemporary figures as Thomas Merton as sources of my pacifist views.

My application was accepted. I joined the US Department of State as a Foreign Service Officer with the aspiration I could contribute to ending the expanding war in Vietnam and to nation-building by appropriate development. I served in Cameroon with two ambassadors, Robert L. Payton (1926–2011) and Lewis Hoffaker (1923–2013), who supported recommendations I made with respect to US foreign policy. Returning to Washington, DC, I served briefly at the State Department, took a leave of absence, and finally resigned.

At the time, I knew little if anything of Merton's writings on contemplation and interfaith relations, nor of controversy that led to an attempt by his superiors to restrain Merton from writing on war. Later, I identified his plight with that of one of my favorite teachers, theologian William Hamilton, who had to resign due to his exploring death of God theology.

Attending CRDS both nourished my increasingly radical theological views, and seeded my interest in Merton, monasticism, and Biblical studies. In "Introduction to Old Testament," taught by Darrell Lance, I wrote an exegetical paper on Micah 6:6–8. In a course with Werner Lemke, I wrote

8. Alinsky, *Rules for Radicals*, 196.

an exegetical paper on the Twenty-third Psalm. In a course with theologian William Hamilton, I wrote a paper entitled "Being Toward the New Humanity: Developing Reflections on Human Freedom in a Cybernetic Society." In an ethics course with Prentiss L. Pemberton, I wrote a paper titled "Deranged Stations on the Road to Confusion: Berkeley and the New Left."

In a course on modern Roman Catholicism with church history professor Winthrop S. Hudson, we read "Problems and Prospects" in which Merton mentioned the renewal of primitive Benedictine communities like Mount Saviour Monastery. Developments in the 1950s exemplified an emerging trend that culminated in the Vatican II reforms.

> The keynotes of the new monasticism was a simple, natural, more or less hard life in contact with nature, nourished by the Bible, the monastic fathers and the liturgy, and faithful to the ancient ideal of prayer, silence and that "holy leisure" (*optium sanctum*) necessary for a pure and tranquil heart in which God could be experienced, tasted, in the silence and freedom of the monk's inner peace . . . the older monasteries soon began in various ways to imitate them and attempt changes along lines which the Primitive Benedictine experiments had suggested. Thus even before the Council decree *Perfectae Caritatis* all the monks were working more or less at renewal.[9]

Hudson encouraged me to do a retreat at Mount Saviour Monastery in Pine City, New York, and to study at the University of Chicago. I did both. Monasticism figured prominently in courses surveying Christian history: early (Robert M. Grant), medieval (Bernard McGinn), reformation (Jerald C. Brauer), and modern (Martin E. Marty). For the Master of Arts degree, I wrote a paper for Professor McGinn on Bernard of Clairvaux's Song of Solomon sermons.

On April 4, 2006, in a lecture at Rhodes College in Memphis, Tennessee, I reconnected with Professor McGinn. Discussing "Why Monasticism Matters," McGinn cited Merton's talk in Calcutta, India, on October 23, 1968: "In speaking for monks I am really speaking for a very strange kind of person, a marginal person."[10] McGinn noted that monks were like hippies and poets and the desert mothers and fathers of early Christianity. Despite their geographic isolation, monks gave themselves entirely to God. McGinn underscored that monks such as Merton united contemplation, action, and freedom to be for the world while yet apart.

---

9. Merton, *Contemplation in a World of Action*, 31–32.

10. Merton, *Asian Journal*, 305.

In 1996, shortly after I moved to Memphis, I attended a conference at Asbury Theological Seminary in Wilmore, Kentucky. A colleague with whom I briefly taught at Central Michigan University in Mount Pleasant, Michigan, offered to drive to Gethsemani, about seventy miles away. We arranged a visit during which we attended one of the Daily Offices. We walked the grounds, stopping at a remarkable group of statues donated in memory of Jonathan M. Daniels, an Episcopal seminarian murdered in 1965 while registering black voters. Journaling, I noted it was a beautiful day, a wonderful drive, and a peaceful place.

I learned that E. Glenn Hinson, who taught church history at Southern Baptist Theological Seminary in Louisville, had met and befriended Merton. Hinson offered a course for students to do a retreat at Gethsemani. After the conference, I introduced a similar course entitled "Merton, Monasticism, and Religious Pluralism." On one occasion, I met Hinson, who explained, "I may have been the first to take a class to Gethsemani in November 1960. My initial interest was to introduce students to medieval Christianity through a visit to the monastery. Merton, who was at the time novice master, did the presentation. He greeted the group wearing what I came to recognize as his customary monastery denim work clothes, looking like any farmer."[11]

In the early 1960s, Protestant seminarians began visiting Gethsemani regularly.[12] Hinson and his students may have seeded this significant contribution by Merton to the ecumenical movement. In a journal entry for April 18, 1961, Merton mentioned their coming to Gethsemani.

> A good group from the Southern Baptist Seminary here yesterday. Very good rapport. I liked them very much. An atmosphere of sincerity and understanding. Differences between us not, I think, minimized. Dr. Hinson, a good and sincere person, with some other faculty members, will come down again. We will talk., perhaps, about the Church. I am glad they will come. Yet each time some new arrangement is made, I wonder if I have not committed myself again too much, The hermitage is "for" that. (Really it is "for nothing,") It seems to be part of the game to have people come to the hermitage. A strange, humorous game of God that I cannot quite take seriously. A mystifying game, in which, no doubt, He will make all things well, and very well. But

11. Conversation in Louisville, Kentucky, on August 20, 2002. In an October 30, 1961 journal entry, Merton mentioned having spoken briefly about peace with a group of church history students during a visit to Gethsemani. Merton, *Turning toward the World*, 175. Jim Forest, Gordon Oyer, Edward Rice, and other Merton biographers confirm Hinson's description.

12. O'Hare, "Thomas Merton and Educative Dialogue."

I must not play it too madly, or become too engrossed in it. It is the game of another, not mine.[13]

Hinson made a crucial point about Merton's ongoing importance.

Merton was taking part in a critical phase of an ecumenical revolution set in motion by Pope John XXIII. Initially, Merton was far from ready for this revolution. But after what he called his "submarine earthquake" in 1949 and 1950, he lent himself in a remarkable way to it. He embodied it in his own personality and outlook, and, in his commitment to Catholic tradition, gave it an anchor to which others could hold. He helped them to see that true ecumenism must occur at the deepest levels of human experience if it is to be unafraid.[14]

In the summer of 1997, I offered the Merton course the first time, and subsequently seven more times. In the syllabus, I prepared students for their experience in a "personal note":

I first started reading Merton in the 1960s. Like millions (literally) of readers, I was familiar with his monastic writings. However, it was his writings after 1958, after his epiphany at the corner of Fourth and Walnut in Louisville, that most influenced me. Merton's defining moment brought him to a deeper identification with humanity and led him to become an agent for justice, racial reconciliation, peace and Christian-Buddhist dialogue. His meetings with D. T. Suzuki, Thich Nhat Hanh, the Dalai Lama, and other Buddhists bore fruit in writings that prompted the Zen scholar Suzuki to identify Merton as the leading interpreter of Asian religions in the West.

Tragically, Merton died by accidental electrocution on December 10, 1968 (the dame day as theologian Karl Barth) during a conference of Catholic and Buddhist monks. In his address to the conference that day, he stated, "The monk is essentially someone who takes up a critical attitude toward the world and its structures, just as these students identify themselves essentially as people who have taken up a critical attitude toward the contemporary world and its structures . . . . What is essential in the monastic life is not embedded in buildings, is not embedded in clothing, is not necessarily embedded even in a rule . . . . It is concerned with this business of total inner transformation. All other things serve that end. I am just saying, in other words,

---

13. Merton, *Turning toward the World*, 109.
14. Hinson, "Thomas Merton, My Brother," 89–90.

what Cassian said in the first lecture, on *puritas cordis*, purity of heart, that every monastic observance tends towards that."[15]

Wherever you are on your spiritual journey, I believe such insights as these, and Merton's legacy of writings on spirituality, justice, and Eastern religion, can bring you into contact with a fellow pilgrim on the road to God. Though those who follow the monastic road are relatively few, more and more pilgrims are finding their way to settings such as Gethsemani and Laretto as a kind of compass. May it be for each of you.

The course included introductory sessions. On Monday of the second week, we journeyed to Gethsemani (men) or Knob's Haven of the Sisters of Loretto in Nerinckx, Kentucky (women) in time to join the monks or sisters who pray the Psalms according to the schedule:

3 15 a.m. Vigils

5:45 a.m. Lauds

6:15 a.m. Eucharist

7:30 a.m. Terce

12:15 p.m. Sext

2:15 p.m. None

5:30 p.m. Vespers

7:30 p.m. Compline.

Merton emphasized the importance of the Psalms. In *Praying the Psalms*, Merton wrote, "There is no aspect of the interior life, no kind of religious experience, no spiritual need . . . that is not depicted and lived out in the Psalms."[16]

In "Psalms and Contemplation," which opens *Bread in the Wilderness*, Merton observed,

> In saying that the Divine Office, the "work of God," held a central and dominant position in the monk's daily life, St. Benedict was only reaffirming the truth that the monk came to the monastery to seek God. The term *"opus Dei"* (work of God), signifies the chanting of the canonical hours—the prayer of the monastic community. This choral office is made up above all of Psalms . . . .

15. Merton, *Asian Journal*, 329, 340.

16. Merton, *Praying the Psalms*, 44.

> The value of the work of God, the *opus Dei* lies not so much
> in the fact that it is a work or a service (*opus*), but in the fact that
> it is a service *of God*.[17]

Benedict wrote *RB*, which has proved durable over the centuries and provides that strangers "be received as Christ himself."[18] As guests, we observed silence at the monastery. Apart from emergencies, I made myself available for an hour under a tree near the entrance to address any problems or questions that had arisen. Some worked with the monks. In early December, a busy time, the monks welcomed assistance helping to fill orders for cheese, fruitcakes, or fudge. For years, sale of such products has generated income for the monks. In advance of our time at Gethsemani, I arranged for the retreat master to meet with the group. Daily after Compline Matthew Kelty (1915–2011), onetime confessor for Merton, gave a talk. By wit and wisdom, Kelty provided a window into the monastic life and Merton.[19]

On Friday noon, we departed for our respective homes. Many of us were traveling together in a van. This provided an opportunity for students to share their experience on retreat. At one point, large hailstones pounded the vehicle so intensely that we could not continue. Consequently, we stopped under an overpass and climbed out of the vehicle to wait out the storm. Like the tsunami we were experiencing, students shared an overflow of God's all-powerful presence in their lives.

During the following week, when we reconvened as a class, students presented tangible expressions of their time at the monastery. Some chose to express their experience in art, music, photographs, or a research paper. Since this was our final session together as a class, I encouraged everyone to incorporate into their routines daily time for spiritual reflection and to do an annual retreat somewhere.

Students resonated with Merton's insight, "The function of the monastic life is to open up [the heart], this deepest center where our human person opens out into the mystery of God."[20] This passage communicated an outcome for me and many students. The time at Gethsemani had tapped into an implicit discontent with society and church as widely constituted. We resonated with a point that Merton in a talk celebrating the 150th

---

17. Merton, *Bread in the Wilderness*, 12–13, Merton's emphasis.

18. Chadwick, *Western Asceticism*, 324, citing the *Rule of Saint Benedict* 53, "The Manner of Entertaining Guests."

19. Sprinkle, "Fr. Matthew Kelty, OCSO, Passes Away"; Matthew Kelty, OCSO, interviewed at the Abbey of Our Lady of Gethsemani in 1997 and 1999.

20. Merton, *Monastic Observances*, 182.

anniversary of the founding of the Congregation of the Sisters of Loretto, 1812–1962. At the time, he said,

> In Christ, God has revealed to us divine love, divine truth, and the divine will; and we have accepted this revelation by freely choosing to be loyal to Christ and his Church in prosperity and adversity, war and peace, in freedom or in prison. This loyalty is the price and guarantee of the only true freedom, and it is on this ideal that the culture of the Christian West has been built. Now that the West has rejected this ideal, and forfeited its spiritual inheritance, the task of those consecrated to God in religion becomes increasingly difficult. The difficulty itself is, then, essential to our vocation. Only by accepting the fact that we are in some sense exiles at odds with materialism, commercialism, and secularism can we begin to be fully faithful to Christ. We must sometimes be resolutely unfashionable, both in morals and in intelligence. This does not mean a cult of anachronism; on the contrary, it is a kind of dissent which is necessary for genuine growth. And Christian dissent is all the more essential as we enter what C. S. Lewis has called the *post-Christian* era.[21]

This passage has described the experience of those who read Merton or attend ITMS gatherings. We have found light along our path to seek to live in ways faithful to the Holy One. Merton biographer Jim Forest summarized this aspect of Merton's life and witness:

> Merton's message was one of freedom, freedom from cultures and mind-styles that have been driven mad with acceleration (he would have been happy to wear a Speed Kills button), freedom to see and hear without self-imposed biases. He hoped for denationalization of the head. Those who have providentially been stirred to be- come the leaven of change, he said, those who seek to renew human imagination, those who try to use their lives to give meaning to communion and community, love, hope and happiness, they most of all must have entered into a peace, a nowness, in which moments, men and events can be savored.[22]

Consistently, more students sought to enroll in the course than the monastery could accommodate. Over the years, eighty-one students

21. Merton, *Springs of Contemplation*, 206, Merton's emphasis.

22. Forest, "Gift of Merton," para. 20. He is a biographer of Merton, and I first interviewed him in Alkmaar, Holland. In 2007 Jim was a keynote speaker at a gathering of the International Thomas Merton Society at Christian Brothers University in Memphis, Tennessee. The conferee took place from June 7–10 on the theme "Wide Open to Heaven and Earth: Contemplation, Community, Culture."

registered. In some instances, students did a retreat closer to home, for example, at Subiaco Abbey, a Benedictine monastery in Arkansas, or at Saint Bernard Abbey in Alabama. Several expressed gratitude for the opportunity the course created to recognize and act on a need for a deep spiritual grounding of their inward and outward journeys.

I owe this phrase to Elizabeth O'Connor. Author of books about The Church of the Saviour in Washington, DC, she commented in my copy of her *Journey Inward, Journey Outward* as follows: "To Paul, who is on both these journeys. Faithfully, Betty O'Connor." During my years teaching at MTS, my partner Nancy and I shared in a servant leadership program inspired by The Church of the Saviour.

Nancy and I have incorporated times of silence, solitude, and stillness in our daily lives. We are active with the Hamilton Monthly Meeting of the Religious Society of Friends (Quakers), which organizes an annual retreat. As well, since 1998, we have spent meaningful time in Australia with the Community of the Transfiguration.[23] We have been blessed by times at the Ignatius Jesuit Centre in Guelph; Ontario; The Sisterhood of St. John the Divine in Toronto, Ontario; St. John's Abbey, a Benedictine monastery in Collegeville, Minnesota; Genesee Abbey, a Cistercian monastery in Piford, New York;[24] and Our Lady of Guadalupe Trappist Abbey in Carlton, Oregon, where Brother Mark Filut, OCSO, welcomed me.[25]

In 2018, I was on my tenth retreat at Gethsemani, about forty miles south from Louisville, Kentucky, where I was doing research for this book. Brother Paul Quenon gifted me with a copy of his book, *In Praise of the Useless Life. A Monk's Memoir.* On the title page, Brother Paul wrote, "For Paul Dekar, may you find a new way of praise in this book." The Epilogue recalled a question Thomas Merton once posed to a group of novice monks. "Did you get what you wanted when you came to the monastery?"

Walking a trail, I paused at a ramshackle hut where retreatants sometimes stop and comment in a guest book. A couple months earlier, a retreatant named Kelly had written, "I don't know that I can believe in the literal biblical story of God, but I do know that I found Him here." I too found God. More accurately, God found me.

---

23. My *Community of the Transfiguration: Journey of a New Monastic Community* introduces the group.

24. On retreat at Genesee Abbey on February 26, 2011, I discussed Merton with James Almeter, mentioned by Henri J. M. Nouwen in *Genesee Diary*, 91, 153. Brother James gifted me with prayers by Luisa Piccarreta, a third-order Dominican.

25. Brother Filut (1933–2020) regularly attended ITMS gatherings. A brief biography is in the spring 2020 *ITMS Newsletter.*

During my first retreat at Gethsemani, I enquired if Brother Patrick Hart was available. I sent a note through the guest master. Later that day, a monk tapped me on the shoulder while I was eating in the retreatants' dining area. Brother Hart whispered to me, "I know a place where we can talk."

Brother Hart encouraged me to do some research about Merton. He suggested that the theme of technology might be productive. He also mentioned that, since 1997, the Shannon Fellowship Committee of ITMS has provided funding to facilitate research at the Merton archives. Brother Hart suggested that I should apply for a Shannon Fellowship. I did. Brother Hart and Donald Grayston, priest of the Anglican diocese of New Westminster, British Columbia, future (2007–9) president of ITMS and a long-time friend, wrote letters on my behalf. Both have died since publication of my earlier book on Merton.

Research supported by my first Shannon Fellowship, in 2003, contributed to an earlier book, *Thomas Merton: Twentieth Century Wisdom for Twenty-First Century Living*. A second Shannon Fellowship, in 2018, contributed to the research for this book.

I thank editors and publishers who have graciously allowed me to reprint previously published articles in this book. The bibliography documents titles, including those cited in notes. *The Thomas Merton Encyclopedia*, v–ix, and *Thomas Merton: Essential Writings*, 11–14, have a chronology of Merton's life and works.

Since 2003, I have attended eleven ITMS gatherings. Each has offered a unique blend of spiritual nurture, academic stimulation, and friendship. In her analysis of these conferences from 1989 to 2013, Patricia A. Burton identified categories that mirror themes in this book.

Two former presidents and several ITMS members have encouraged my reading, writing, and teaching about Merton. I am especially grateful to Christine M. Bochen, seventh ITMS president and Professor Emerita of Religious Studies, Nazareth College, Rochester, New York, who has written a Foreword. Her presidential address "*Mercy within Mercy within Mercy*" is available on the ITMS website. Her title draws on a remarkable passage entitled "Fire Watch, July 4, 1952." Merton records the voice of God in paradise, "*I have always overshadowed Jonas with my mercy and cruelty I know not at all. Have you had sight of Me, Jonas, My child? Mercy within mercy within mercy. I have forgiven the universe without end, because I have never known sin.*"[26]

---

26. "Fire Watch, July 4, 1952," is the epilogue of Merton, *Sign of Jonas*, 351–52, Merton's emphasis. Lawrence S. Cunningham included it in Merton, *Thomas Merton, Spiritual Master*, 119.

I am equally grateful to Mark C. Meade, sixteenth ITMS president and TMC Associate Director at Bellarmine University in Louisville, where I have twice benefitted from help provided by Mark and Paul M. Pearson. Mark has written an Afterword. His presidential talk, "The Reality of Personal Relationships Saves Everything," is also available on the ITMS website.

Among ITMS members, some are friends for long standing such as Bill Apel, emeritus professor of religious studies at Linfield College, McMinnville, Oregon. Bill signed my copy of his *Signs of Peace: The Interfaith Letters of Thomas Merton* as follows: "To someone who for me is not only a friend but a sign of peace." Allan McMillan, a Catholic priest now living in Brantford, Ontario, has encouraged me throughout bringing this book to fruition. As well, Stacy Li, Allan McMillan, Ron Morissey, and John Porter have read and commented on book chapters.

In addition to Brother Hart, I have personally known several persons significant in Merton's journey including Mark Van Doren, Nhat Hanh, and Catharine de Hueck Doherty. Van Doren supervised Merton's graduate studies at Columbia University. He also taught at the University of California, Berkeley, where I had a course with him on modern British literature.

In New York City during the summer of 1941, Merton worked with Doherty, a Russian-born aristocrat who combined deep spirituality with a commitment to social justice. In 1947, she founded the Madonna House Apostolate in Cambermere, Ontario. A Christian community of lay men, women, and priests dedicated to loving and serving Jesus Christ, members have observed the Little Mandate, which reads,

> Arise—go! Sell all you possess.
>
> Give it directly, personally to the poor.
>
> Take up My cross (their cross) and follow Me,
>
> going to the poor, being poor,
>
> being one with them, one with Me.
>
> Little—be always little! Be simple, poor, childlike.
>
> Preach the Gospel with your life—without compromise!
>
> Listen to the Spirit. He will lead you.
>
> Do little things exceedingly well for love of Me.
>
> Love . . . love . . . love, never counting the cost.
>
> Go into the marketplace and stay with Me.
>
> Pray, fast. Pray always, fast.

Be hidden. Be a light to your neighbor's feet.

Go without fears into the depths of men's hearts. I shall be with you.

Pray always. I will be your rest.[27]

During the 1980s, I did two retreats at Madonna House where Catharine encouraged me to return to the Russian Orthodox Church in which I was baptized and raised. This has led me to undertake several retreats at Orthodox monasteries, and to attend the Easter service at an Orthodox congregation. Over the years, Merton corresponded with her. The Catholic Church has considered her canonization.

In early 2002, I invited friends to explore bringing Nhat Hanh to Memphis. He accepted our invitation along with forty members of his community. On September 28, 2002 in Memphis, Tennessee, several thousand persons gathered at the Lorraine Motel where Martin Luther King Jr. was murdered. Nhat Hanh lit a flame of peace and, with Cao Ngoc Phuong and other spiritual leaders walked ten miles to a mid-city park. What distinguished the walk? Everyone walked in silence. At the park, people ate in silence. Only later, in a public talk, did Nhat Hanh break the silence.

Organized a year after the collapse of the World Trade Center on September 11, 2001, PeaceWalk 2002 manifested a resolve of participants to contribute to building a better world. Later, our Buddhist friends purchased land for a retreat center, Magnolia Village in northern Mississippi, to which Nhat Hanh returned in 2005 for a formal dedication.

Merton met the Vietnamese monk Nhat Hahn on May 28, 1966, and wrote an essay, "Nhat Hanh Is My Brother."[28] Along with Dr. Martin Luther King Jr., Nhat Hanh was to have joined Merton at Gethsemani in April 1968. Dr. King's murder made this impossible. Chapter 8 of this book imagines a conversation that might have ensued during this retreat.

I have organized this book around Micah 6:8. The text highlights emphases of Merton who read Micah within the lectionary, a three-year cycle covering most of the Bible. In 2000, this text shaped the Micah Challenge during the Jubilee and Make Poverty History campaigns that sought to raise a prophetic voice for and with the poor.

A crucial decision concerned our subject's name. The late Michael Mott, who wrote a biography of Merton, mentioned nearly fifty names, including his monastic name, Father Louis. I follow the name Merton

27. Doherty, *Poustinia*, 204. William Shannon wrote an entry about her in Shannon et al., *Thomas Merton Encyclopedia*, 118.

28. In Buddhism, Thich is an honorific title like Reverend, as in the Reverend Dr. Martin Luther King Jr.

preferred. In a letter to Naomi Burton, friend and literary agent, Merton wrote, "So if I sign frater Louis it means Tom."[29]

Quoting Scripture, I have used the New Revised Standard Version. Quoting Merton can be a challenge. In journals or correspondence, Merton mentioned drafts of books that sometimes appeared under different titles. Frequently, he also rewrote material. *What Is Contemplation?* (1948) grew into *The Inner Experience* (2003). *Seeds of Contemplation* (1949) became *New Seeds of Contemplation* (1961), chapter 16 of which, "The Root of War Is Fear," was first published in the October 1961 issue of *The Catholic Worker*.

I write with attention to gender. "Monk" refers to male monastics, "nun" to female monastics. If a citation is not inclusive, I follow the original texts of Merton and contemporaries who adopted the literary conventions of the forties, fifties, and sixties. In "Hagia Sophia," a prose poem first published in 1962, Merton was more inclusive in language. If, two generations later, Merton were still writing, I trust that he would use non-gender-specific prose.

Prayerfully, I offer this book to the Holy One, who is Sovereign pulsing in and through me, whose Truth is greater than disaster and whose Peace silences all counter evidence.[30]

29. Mott, *Seven Mountains of Thomas Merton*, 7, 235 and Shannon, "Naomi Burton Stone," 452–53.

30. Paraphrase from Merton's "Senescente Mundo," *The Tears of the Blind Lions* (1949), *Collected Poems*, 222.

Section One: **Doing Justice**

Introduction

A FEW YEARS AGO for another book, at the British Library in London, England, I read a speech that Victor Hugo gave in December 1849 at an International Peace Congress. Hugo stated that peace, a universal religious ideal, emanated from divine law. For Hugo, God's dream was peace, not war; justice, not oppression; universal prosperity, not the gap between rich and poor that characterized the economic imbalance between the rich and poor in Hugo's time, and still does. Deploring the immense sums nations squandered on armaments, Hugo urged all countries to direct these funds to the arts, research, agriculture, or science. He pleaded that nations cease to traffic in arms. He advocated creation of international bodies to settle disputes and mediate conflicting interests. As the audience applauded, Hugo said,

> The divine law is not one of war, but peace. Lay down your arms. And in that day you will all have one common thought, common interests, a common destiny; you will embrace each other and recognize each other as children of the same blood and of the same race; that day you will be a people, costs directed not to arms but the common good.[1]

In 1862, Hugo embedded his vision in *Les Misérables*. The novel has inspired many film, television, and theater adaptations. A 1980 stage production of *Les Misérables* ended,

> For the wretched of the earth,
> There is a flame that never dies.
> Even the darkest night will end
> And the sun will rise

---

1. The chapters in this section draw on "Practices of Jubilee," in my *Holy Boldness*. For the Hugo speech: Hugo, "Speech of Victor Hugo."

3

They will live again in freedom
In the garden of the Lord.[2]

These stirring lines recall the image of Eden restored. In Revelation 22:1–2, John describes the river of life rising from the throne of God and of the Lamb and flowing crystal clear. Down the middle of the city street, on either bank of the river, is the tree of life, the leaves of which are for the healing of the nations.

Les Misérables evokes the biblical understanding of justice. In Hebrew, the word *tsedeq* (righteousness) and in Greek *dikalosume* (observance of God's law) refer to equitable, impartial behavior by people in society.[3] In Leviticus 25, biblical justice is manifest in jubilee practices. Every seventh year, land is to have a sabbatical. If the land is left to rest yet crops are produced, harvests are to be prioritized to feed people in need. During a jubilee year, seven times seven years plus one, God's people are to return land taken illegitimately to the original owner and to free slaves.

As recorded in Luke 4:18–19, Jesus speaks of the jubilee principle, announcing that the Lord had anointed him "to bring good news to the poor. He has sent me to proclaim release to the captives and recovery of sight to the blind, to let the oppressed go free, and to proclaim the year of the Lord's favor." Mark 10:17–22 records Jesus telling a rich man to give to the poor. Another text, 2 Peter 1:1–7, describes the path Jesus wanted, and still wants people to walk:

> Simeon Peter, a servant and apostle of Jesus Christ, To those who have received a faith as precious as ours through the righteousness of our God and Savior Jesus Christ: May grace and peace be yours in abundance in the knowledge of God and of Jesus our Lord. His divine power has given us everything needed for life and godliness, through the knowledge of him who called us by his own glory and goodness. Thus he has given us, through these things, his precious and very great promises, so that through them you may escape from the corruption that is in the world because of lust, and may become participants of the divine nature. For this very reason, you must make every effort to support your faith with goodness, and goodness with knowledge, and knowledge with self-control, and self-control with endurance, and endurance with godliness, and godliness with mutual affection, and mutual affection with love.

2. From the finale of the 1980 stage production of *Les Misérables*, a musical by Alain Boublil and Claude-Michele Schönberg, lyrics by Herbert Kretzmer.

3. "Righteousness in the OT," by E. R. Achtemeier, and "Righteousness in the NT," by P. J. Achtemeier, in *The Interpreter's Dictionary of the Bible, R–Z* (1962).

Early in the third millennium, Micah, Jesus, and all biblical writers still call upon God's people to do justice. This requires meeting basic needs of those on social assistance. God's people are to resettle refugees from Rwanda, Syria, Turkey, Yemen, or other conflict zones; to alleviate suffering by women (or men) and children in domestic abuse to find safety, security, and means to rebuild their lives in a new home; to fill food banks; and to address other appeals for social assistance.

On an international level, doing justice requires attending to the needs of the world's poor. As an example, during the year 2000, I participated in an international jubilee movement working for the forgiveness or cancellation of crushing debts of impoverished countries owed to the world's most powerful countries and organizations like the World Bank and International Monetary Fund. A pamphlet of the movement cited Dr. Martin Luther King Jr., as follows:

> Any religion that professes to be concerned with the souls of persons and is not concerned with the slums that damn them, the economic conditions that strangle them, and the social conditions that cripple them is dry-as-dust religion. We must come to see that the whole Jericho Road must be transformed so that men and women will not be constantly beaten and robbed as they make their way on life's highway . . . an edifice which produces beggars needs restructuring.[4]

Our time, the mid-twenty-first century, is the right time to ensure that everyone has what is necessary for self-sufficiency and security. Our time is the right time to restructure social systems, especially in the rich North, in ways that eliminate beggars. In short, our time is the right time to honor the call of Micah and Jesus to do justice by prioritizing the needs of those most in need.

In this chapter, I have revisited two articles that explore this call to do justice. The first, "Technology and the Loss of Paradise," initially appeared in *Thomas Merton: Monk on the Edge*, edited by Ross Labrie and Angus Stuart (North Vancouver: Thomas Merton Society of Canada, 2012). The second, "God's Messenger: Thomas Merton on Racial Justice," was published in *The Merton Annual* 32 (2019) 137–54.

---

4. Quoted from a brochure entitled "Proclaim Jubilee: Poor Country Debt and Economic Justice, Belmont University Delegation to Nicaragua and Washington, D. C, May 21–June 5, 2000."

1

Technology and the Loss of Paradise

ON JUNE 5, 1966, Thomas Merton gave a talk, "The Christian in a Technological World," to novices at the Abbey of Gethsemani.[1] At the time, Merton was spending more and more time at a hermitage near the main compound. In October 1964, he received permission to sleep at St. Mary of Carmel "without any special restriction." Merton experienced himself as "fully human . . . . Fit to be offered to God" and as free to explore life in Christ. Like the holy men and women who went to the wilderness in the fourth century, Merton was seeking his own true self, or inner self in Christ.[2]

The hermitage was paradise on earth where he could recover his truest self. By paradise, Merton had in mind a state . . . a place, on earth . . . in which man was originally created to live on earth . . . . What the Desert Fathers sought when they believed they could find "paradise" in the desert was the lost innocence, the emptiness and purity of heart which had belonged to Adam and Eve in Eden.

With the desert saints, Merton understood his calling as growing in love. His ultimate goal was neither love, nor purity of heart. Rather, "the ultimate end was the "Kingdom of God." With Staretz Zosima, Merton believed "paradise is attainable because . . . it is present within us and we have only to discover it there."[3]

In an essay entitled "Rain and the Rhinoceros," Merton cited the provocative nineteenth-century writer and thinker Henry David Thoreau, who spent two years in a self-built house on the shores of Walden Pond outside of

---

1. The full text of "The Christian in a Technological World" may be found in my earlier book, *Thomas Merton: Twentieth-Century Wisdom for Twenty-First-Century Living*, 205–13.

2. Merton, *Wisdom of the Desert*, 3–5.

3. Merton, *Zen and the Birds of Appetite*, 116. In a Russian Orthodox monastery, a staretz is a wise elder.

Concord, Massachusetts. Thoreau was likely as self-aware a prophet as Merton. Both warned future generations of the capacity of technology, wrongly used, to distract, inhibit, and undermine one's quest to recover paradise lost.

> Thoreau sat in *his* cabin and criticized the railways. I sit in mine and wonder about a world that has, well, progressed. I must read *Walden* again, and see if Thoreau already guessed that he was part of what he thought he could escape. But it is not a matter of "escaping." It is not even a matter of protesting very audibly. Technology is here, even in the cabin. True, the utility line is not here yet, and so G.E. is not here yet either. When the utilities and G.E. enter my cabin arm in arm it will be nobody's fault but my own. I admit it. I am not kidding anybody, even myself. I will suffer their bluff and patronizing complacencies in silence. I will let them think they know what I am doing here . . . .
>
> Of course at three-thirty A.M. the SAC plane goes over, red light winking low under the clouds, skimming the wooded summits on the south side of the valley, loaded with strong medicine. Very strong. Strong enough to burn up all these woods and stretch our hours of fun into eternities.[4]

This excerpt indicated Merton's concern less with his personal life and more with human rights, warfare, and the natural world. Technology impacted each area. Regarding to nature, Merton expressed concern that people used technology to alter the natural environment, changing it into an artificial one without due regard for unintended consequences.

From 1955 to 1965, Merton served as Master of Novices at Gethsemani, after which he moved permanently to his hermitage. There, he occasionally received guests or gave a talk. In his June 5, 1966 talk, Merton cited concrete examples of useful technological innovation:

> OK, fine, there is nothing wrong with lawn mowers; monastic life allows us to do the lawns. This is excellent, but this is technology. Technological society around a place like this makes possible a lot of closely cropped grass.
>
> Another example is that we used to have many creeks and fields around here. Of course we have rains and then there are many more. This is what happens. Instead of five fields, you have one; instead of several creeks, you have one. Of course it sometimes rains then you have many. But that's exactly how technology operates, so you can simplify everything and get at it faster. The ancient monastic outlook on things is suspicious of this view of the world. A person may ask if this is practical. I don't know.

4. Merton, *Raids on the Unspeakable*, 12–13, 14, Merton's emphasis.

Attempts to control nature troubled Merton. Lack of concern about a crucial effect of technology especially bothered him. As antidote to the tendency not to question confidence in machines, Merton called on humans to accept limits, to use technology rightly, and to work for a "better world."[5] Merton saw "paradise is all around us," but lamented,

> we do not understand. It is wide open. The sword is taken away, but we do not know it: we are off 'one to his farm and another to his merchandise.' [Matt. 22: 5] Lights on. Clocks ticking. Thermostats working. Stoves cooking. Electric shavers filling radios with static. 'Wisdom' cries the dawn deacon, but we do not attend.[6]

Merton made careful observations about the seasons, the elements, plants, and creatures. Emphasizing the intrinsic worth of creation and of the possible loss of our right relationship to nature, Merton wrote that humans are part of nature.

In an April 11, 1963 journal entry, Merton described having come upon a titmouse, a small resident bird. It lay dead on the grass, perhaps due to his actions. Merton had dumped some calcium chloride on a couple anthills intending to direct the ants elsewhere, not to poison them. Merton lamented, "What a miserable bundle of foolish idiots we are! We kill everything around us even when we think we love and respect nature and life. This sudden power to deal death all around us simply by the way we live, and in total "innocence" and "ignorance," is by far the most disturbing symptom of our time."[7] He journaled,

> Two superb days. When was there ever such a morning as yesterday? Cold at first, the hermitage dark in the moonlight (I had permission to go up right after Lauds), a fire in the grate (and how beautifully firelight shines through the lattice-blocks and all through the house at night!) Then the sunrise, enormous yolk of energy spreading and spreading as if to take over the sky. After that the ceremonies of the birds feeding in the dewy grass and the meadowlark feeding and singing. Then the quiet, totally silent day, warm, mild morning under the climbing sun. It was hard to say psalms: one's attention was totally absorbed by the great arc of the sky and the trees and hills and grass and all things in them. How absolutely true, and how central a truth, that we are simply part of nature, though we are the part

---

5. Merton, *Contemplation in a World of Action*, 148.

6. Merton, *Conjectures of a Guilty Bystander*, 132.

7. Merton, *Turning toward the World*, 312, Merton's emphasis.

which recognizes God. It is not Christianity, indeed, but post-Cartesian technologism that separates man from the world and makes him a kind of little god in his own right, with his clear ideas, all by himself.

We have to be humbly and realistically what we are, and the denial of it results only in the madness and cruelties of Nazism, or of the people who are sick with junk and drugs. And one can be "part of nature" surely, without being Lady Chatterley's lover.[8]

Reflecting on implications of such experiences, Merton called on people to acknowledge how well God has made all things. Affirming the sacredness of all life, he concluded that denial of our place in nature resulted in the madness and cruelties of Nazism, in people becoming sick with junk or drugs, and in the loss of paradise. Merton respected other writers who championed taking everyday care of earth. He pointed to the investigations of scientists like Rachel Carson (1907–64), author of groundbreaking books that challenged readers to reclaim their proper place in paradise.

Carson's celebrated *Silent Spring* was first serialized in *The New Yorker*. She dedicated the book to Albert Schweitzer (1875–1965), humanitarian, medical missionary, and, in 1952, recipient of the Nobel Peace Prize. In her dedication, Carson cited Schweitzer as saying, "Man has lost his capacity to foresee and to forestall. He will end by destroying the earth." Carson called for new, imaginative, creative ways to share earth with one another and all creation. As much as any piece of writing can be credited, *Silent Spring* inspired birth of the modern environmental movement and passage by US Congress of legislation to care for earth. A commentator observed, "*Silent Spring* changed the world by describing it."[9]

Through a friend, Anne Ford, Merton secured a copy of *Silent Spring*. After reading the book, Merton wrote Carson to commend her for "contributing a most valuable and essential piece of evidence for the diagnosis of the ills of our civilization." Merton observed, "The awful irresponsibility with which we scorn the smallest values is part of the same portentous irresponsibility with which we dare to use our titanic power in a way that threatens not only civilization but life itself." He saw the need to address a "*consistent pattern*" that runs through every aspect of life—culture, economy, "our whole way of life"—and to arrive at a "clear cogent statement of our life, so that we may begin to correct them." Otherwise, humans might direct their efforts to superficial symptoms only. This risked aggravating the sickness in that the "*remedies*" became "*expressions of the*

8. Merton, *Turning toward the World*, 312, Merton's emphasis.
9. Kolbert, "Human Nature," 23.

sickness itself." Merton characterized the root cause of the problem as a subconscious hatred of life and a death wish.[10]

There is no evidence that Carson received the letter, or replied. Merton wrote to her before he kept letters he received or copies of letters he wrote. In this case, he kept a carbon planning to use it in *Cold War Letters*. Merton's superiors forbade him to publish the book, which did not appear in his lifetime.[11]

Merton's letter to Carson reflected not only his growing concern about the impact of technology on nature, but also his self-understanding as monk and writer. In *Thoughts in Solitude*, Merton wrote that some technological advances undermined one's true humanity.

> When men are merely submerged in a mass of impersonal human beings pushed around by automatic forces, they lose their true humanity, their integrity, their ability to love, their capacity for self-determination . . . . No amount of technological progress will cure the hatred that eats away the vitals of materialistic society like a spiritual cancer. The only cure is, and must always be, spiritual. There is not much use talking to men about God and love if they are not able to listen.[12]

Merton recognized that our devices had become like angels—or the devil—something in the realm of the sacred that had come to stand between us and the real world. A characteristic of modernity that troubled Merton was a lack of awareness of this numbing of the spiritual dimension of human beings.

In a poem entitled "Exploits of a Machine Age," Merton captures the emptiness of modern, technological society. A couple awakens one morning, again dismayed

> By their own thin faces in the morning. They
>
> Hoped they would not die today, either.
>
> They hoped for some light
>
> Breakfast and a steady hand.

The couple flee to their "protected work" and "unsafe machinery" by which they lived empty lives while their employers lived well. At the end of the day, the machines are safe, nothing at all having happened. Literally

---

10. Merton to Carson, January 12, 1963, in Merton, *Witness to Freedom*, 70–72.

11. In 2006, Orbis Books published *Cold War Letters*, edited by Christine M. Bochen and William H. Shannon.

12. Merton, *Thoughts in Solitude*, xii.

nothing. The couple return to their grim dwellings, "muttering." "Better luck tomorrow!"[13]

Merton drew on important twentieth-century thinkers, including writer Albert Camus (1913–60), mentioned often in Merton's journals and essays, and sociologist Émile Durkheim (1858–1917) who characterized modern people as living at loose ends, a treadmill-like existence called *anomie*. For Merton, this constituted formless living driven by an insatiable will, a sort of derangement.

Merton explained that technology was not in itself opposed to spirituality or to religion. Rather, technology had become a great and dangerous temptation. Merton warned that there can be "a deadening of spirit and of sensibility, a blunting of perception, a loss of awareness, a lowering of tone, a general fatigue and lassitude, a proneness to unrest and guilt which we might be less likely to suffer if we simply went out and worked with our hands in the woods or the fields." Merton invoked the possibility that good means could result in bad ends. As a result, he insisted on the need for "a certain prudence . . . in the use of machines."

For Merton, it was imperative to leave to God the sanctification of our own nature, "the temple of our being." Technology could fulfill its promise only by serving all that is higher than itself—reason, humankind, God. "But becoming autonomous, existing only for itself, it [technology] imposes upon man its own irrational demands, and threatens to destroy him. Let us hope it is not too late for man to regain control."[14]

This awareness sustained Merton, who faithfully observed the spiritual disciplines of Benedictine monasticism, including meditation, confession, and the Liturgy of the Hours. Such practices enabled Christians to *"reach and realize their limit"* while recognizing that their praise and other practices could not "attain to God" but "reach not only the heart of God but also the heart of creation itself, finding everywhere the beauty of the righteousness of Yahweh." [15]

In the passage that followed, Merton highlighted the importance of the "night spirit" and "dawn breath" in restoring to life the forest that has been cut down. Merton cited the Ox Mountain parable of Mencius, who lived during the fourth century before the Common Era in China. Many Chinese regard Mencius as their Second Sage after Confucius.

---

13. Merton, *Collected Poems*, 237–38. The poem first appeared in *The Strange Islands* (1957), a collection dedicated to Mark Van Doren, who supervised Merton's graduate work at the Columbia University, and Dorothy Van Doren.

14. Merton, *Conjectures of a Guilty Bystander*, 25–26, 77.

15. Merton, *Conjectures of a Guilty Bystander*, 136–37.

> Even though the Ox Mountain forest has been cut to the ground,
> if the mountain is left to rest and recuperate in the night and
> the dawn, the trees will return. But men cut them down, cattle
> browse on the new shoots: no night spirit, no dawn breath—no
> rest, no renewal—and finally one is convinced that there never
> were any woods on the Ox Mountain. So, Mencius concludes,
> with human nature. Without the night spirit the dawn breath,
> silence, passivity, rest, man's nature cannot be itself. In its bar-
> renness it is no longer *natuira*: nothing grows from it, nothing is
> born of it any more.[16]

Merton regarded the Ox Mountain story as showing how human nature was created good but later corrupted. For Merton, the story offered parallels with the Abrahamic religions and was important in his quest for a spirituality by which he could satisfy his need for unhurriedness. Having escaped the "busy-ness" of the world, Merton found monastic life too frenetic.

Fascinated by spiritual paths offering alternatives to values of technological culture, Merton looked to aboriginal peoples, those who in his view exemplified the qualities he sought. Merton's Cistercian colleague Matthew Kelty, mentioned in the introduction to this book, was a crucial resource. Kelty had served as missionary in Papau New Guinea from 1947 to 1951. Around 1970, he lived there in a hermitage. In 1982, he returned to Gethsemani.

Kelty had studied cargo cults, messianic movements that appeared sporadically, notably during and immediately after World War II in Papau New Guinea. The aboriginal people saw troops based in their islands importing large quantities of material goods. After the war, the military bases closed, thereby eliminating a source of goods and income. Attempting to gain further deliveries of goods, indigenous people initiated cargo cults in which they engaged in ritualistic practices like building crude landing strips, aircraft, and radio equipment. They imitated behavior and dress of the troops. Merton saw parallels between the cargo cults and themes in apocalyptic literature and other phenomena sweeping the modern world. A universal feature of these social movements was to attack everything old and to create something new.

Merton read *Mambu* by anthropologist Kenelm Burridge and reviewed the book in an essay, "Cargo Cults of the South Pacific." Merton

---

16. Merton, *Conjectures of a Guilty Bystander*, 137. See *Sources of Chinese Tradition* for references to Mencius and the Ox-Bow parable. In my earlier book *Thomas Merton: Twentieth-Century Wisdom for Twenty-First-Century Living*, I devote chapter 6 to Merton on "Care of Earth." Other scholars also highlight Merton's love of nature, including Kathleen Deignan and Monica Weis; also, "Forest Is My Bride."

resonated with Burridge's idea of a New Man, a fusion of white and Kanaka who will get cargo. Merton saw this as paralleling unreal, mythlike expectations regarding technology. Merton concluded this was dangerous.

> If our white Western myth-dream demands of us that we spiritually enslave others in order to "save" them, we should not be surprised when their own myth-dream demands of them that they get entirely free of us to save themselves. But both the white man's and the native's myth-dreams are only partial and inadequate expression of the whole truth. It is not that the primitive needs to be dominated by the white man in order to become fully human. Nor is it that he needs to get rid of the white man. Each needs the other to cooperate in the common enterprise of building a world adequate for the historical maturity of man.[17]

A careful reader of indigenous spiritualties, Merton worried about ongoing devastation by human beings of the natural world. He raised concern about ecological balance, and the need for people to unite technology and wisdom in total self-forgetful creativity and service. "It would however be insufficient to limit Christian obligation, in the present crisis, merely to a course of action that can be somehow reconciled with moral principles. The problem is deeper. What is needed is a social action that will have the power to renew society because it springs *from the inner renewal of the Christian and of his church.*" Merton saw the basic problem of his time as "basically spiritual. One important aspect of this problem is the fact that in many Christians, the Christian conscience seems to function only in rudimentary vestigial faculty, robbed of its full vigor and inescapable of attaining its real purpose: a life completely transformed in Christ."[18]

Merton wrote prior to the publication of writings that have enabled Christians today to recover spiritual practices of Christians in the first and second centuries of the Common Era. For Rita Nakashima Brock and Rebecca Ann Parker, among myriad authors, by the third century Christians had exchanged crucifixion for empire. Brock and Parker believed communities were needed to train perception and teach ethical grace. "Paradise provides deep reservoirs for resistance and joy. It calls us to embrace life's aching tragedies and persistent beauties, to labor for justice and peace, to honor one another's dignity, and to root our lives in the soil of this good and difficult earth."[19]

17. Merton, *Love and Living*, 94.

18. Merton, *Peace in the Post-Christian Era*, 149.

19. Brock and Parker, *Saving Paradise*, 410; also, White, "Historical Roots of Our Ecological Crisis," 1203–7.

Merton's considerable gifts included his call to live respectfully on earth, to leave light footprints, and to relate to communities respectful of the integrity of creation. Merton worried that humans had come to believe technology could fix whatever problems life presented. He sounded an alarm similar to those of the wider global environmental movement that emerged in his lifetime. By April 1970, less than two years after Merton died, more than 300,000 people in the United States, and greater numbers worldwide, took part in Earth Day. At the time, it was the largest environmental demonstration in history.

Writing on April 22, 2020, the fiftieth anniversary of Earth Day, I recognize the extent to which climate catastrophe has intensified the importance of addressing climate change as well as other threats to life on earth. Merton contributed to a growing movement to prioritize care of earth and refusal to identify nationals of countries with which the United States was at war as enemy. On May 26, 1966, a time when the United States was at war with North Vietnam, he met Vietnamese monk Thich Nhat Hanh, whom Merton called his brother.[20]

Merton also called for demilitarizing life by refusing to consent to preparation for what could lead to the destruction of all life in a nuclear war. "Our duty . . . is to help emphasize with all the force in our disposal that the Church earnestly seeks the abolition of war . . . underscore declarations like those of Pope John XXIII pleading with world leaders to renounce force in the settlement of international disputes and confine themselves to negotiations."[21]

Merton called on us to simplify our lives as a step to giving up attachment to the relative prosperity of the United States and the West.[22] Merton understood that humans, having the power to destroy, also had the power and the freedom to nurture, to look beyond the glitter of modern Western society, and to contribute to saving humanity. Debunking the "ethic of expediency and efficiency," decrying nationalism, which he saw as inevitably leading to war, and denouncing all that the automobile had come to represent, Merton believed that "we have created for ourselves a culture that is not yet livable for mankind as a whole." This failure was at the heart of "all contemporary American problems: race, war, the crisis of marriage, the

---

20. Merton, *Passion for Peace*, 260–62.

21. Merton, *Peace in the Post-Christian Era*, 155.

22. Chapter 4, "Thomas Merton on Simplification of Life," in my *Thomas Merton: Twentieth-Century Wisdom*.

flight from reality into myth and fanaticism, the growing brutality and irrationality of American mores."[23]

Not without hope, Merton saw humans as part of a world God had created and pronounced good. Merton believed it possible to channel technology along a better path, contribute to the healing of paradise lost, and restore the integrity of creation.

23. Merton, *Conjectures of a Guilty Bystander*, 73, 76.

2

Thomas Merton on Racial Justice[1]

LET US ACKNOWLEDGE THAT we are on traditional Chochenyo territory. In the eighteenth century, the Chochenyos moved *en masse* to the Mission San Francisco de Assisi, founded in 1776, and Mission San José of Fremont, founded in 1797. Most of the aboriginal population was baptized and educated as Catholics but died from disease. Only a few remained by 1900. In "Ishi: A Meditation," one of his essays on the struggles between North America's colonizers and First Peoples, Merton wrote,

> Genocide is a new word. Perhaps the word is new because technology has not got into the game of destroying whole races at once. The destruction of races is not new—just easier. Nor is it a specialty of totalitarian regimes. We have forgotten that a century ago white America was engaged in the destruction of entire tribes and ethnic groups of Indians.[2]

This chapter highlights Thomas Merton's correspondence during the 1960s with three African American civil rights activists: a priest, August Thompson (1926–2019), the musician Robert Lawrence Williams, and the novelist James Baldwin (1924–87). As well, we highlight several articles by Merton on racial justice. This writing forms a contribution by Merton to racism awareness work that scholars of social movements of the 1960s have tended to ignore.[3] This relative lacuna contrasts with greater attention given

1. This paper was first read at the 16th ITMS General Meeting at Santa Clara University in California. Unpublished manuscripts cited are in the TMC; http://www.merton.org/Research/Correspondence.

2. Merton, *Passion for Peace*, 263.

3. Exceptions include Charters, *Portable Sixties Reader*, 109–18, for Merton's "Original Child Bomb," and O'Connell, "Civil Rights Movement" and "Racism," in *The Thomas Merton Encyclopedia*.

other issues that Merton addressed: ecumenism, environmental justice, technology, and the threat of nuclear war.

Apart from his January 1940 visit to Cuba and experience working in the summer of 1941 at Catharine Doherty's Friendship House in Harlem, and at Columbia University where Merton did his graduate work, Merton had little contact with people of color. This remained the case during Merton's monastic life. In a journal entry, Merton noted the only Negro at Gethsemani was Martin de Porres.[4]

August Thompson was born in Baldwin, Louisiana. In 1957, he was ordained in New Orleans as priest for the Diocese of Alexandria, Louisiana. In October 1963, Thompson visited the Abbey of Gethsemani, where he briefly met Merton one evening. At the time, Thompson was rector of St. Charles Church, Ferriday, Louisiana. Merton journaled,

> New light on the South, again, and how impossible the situation really is. Actually it is quite a unique one for which new formulas must be sought and are being sought. But what will it avail? Whatever will happen if [Barry] Goldwater manages to get himself elected President in 1964.[5]

Subsequently until 1968, Thompson and Merton exchanged letters. Their correspondence dealt with issues such as prospects for elevating an African American to a bishopric and a dialogue with John Howard Griffin (1920–80), who wrote of his travels in the southern United States after having had his skin temporarily darkened. The procedure enabled him to pass as a black man. *Sepia Magazine* financed the project in exchange for the right to print the account as a series of articles. Griffin's journal of his experiences became the genesis of *Black Like Me*.[6]

Edward M. Keating (1925–2003), publisher of *Ramparts*, a Catholic political and literary journal, wrote Merton that he had met "a most interesting Negro who is extremely interested in engaging in a rather unique dialogue, and I immediately thought that you [Merton] would be the ideal

4. Merton, *Dancing in the Water of Life*, 44, entry for December 9, 1963.

5. Merton, *Dancing in the Water of Life*, 30, entry for October 29, 1963. For Thompson, see "Obituary, August Thompson"; Hillis, "Sign of Contradiction"; and Hillis, "Letters to a Black Catholic Priest."

6. Griffin, *Black Like Me*. *Uncommon Vision: The Life and Times of John Howard Griffin* was a film released in 2011 to commemorate the fiftieth anniversary of the book's publication. Merton's estate chose Griffin to write the authorized biography of Merton, but poor health prevented Griffin from extending the project, which appeared in part as *Follow the Ecstasy: Thomas Merton, the Hermitage Years, 1965–1968*. For Merton to Griffin, see Daggy, *Road to Joy*, 131–41. Columbia University houses the original letters.

person to engage in this with him." Subsequently, articles by Thompson and Griffin appeared in the Christmas 1963 issue of the publication. A photo of Thompson with the caption "The Negro and the White Conscience" took up most of the cover. Merton's essay entitled "The Black Revolution: Letters to a White Liberal" was lead article in the issue.[7]

Father Thompson's piece elicited a negative response by his bishop, Charles Pasquale Greco of Alexandria, Louisiana (1894–1987). Greco rebuked Thompson as follows: "the image of Your Mother the Church which you, her son, have projected to the world is unfair, is a disservice to her and has inflicted a deep wound upon her. We pray God [that] we may be able to heal it."[8] On November 26, 1963, four days after the assassination of President John F. Kennedy, Thompson wrote Merton seeking advice on how to respond to Bishop Greco.

In his November 30 reply, Merton advised Thompson to approach the bishop with humility and to state his love, respect, and loyalty for the Church. However, Merton cautioned Thompson not to acquiesce in such a way as could be seen as disloyalty to his own integrity or to Christ. Urging obedience, Merton recommended that Thompson admit, defensively,

> that you may have lacked prudence in expressing these views, but that you felt that you were expressing them fairly. If your feelings in this regard were mistaken, then you are sorry, but you were personally sincere and felt you were doing your duty in saying these things. Then you can express your love, respect and loyalty for the Church, and say this love includes a deep respect for your superiors, in whom you wish to see Christ, but also a love and respect for your fellow Negro Catholics, in whom you also see Christ and to whom you have a responsibility, but end by assuring him that you know obedience comes first, tell him you are extremely sorry for this misunderstanding etc etc. In this way I think you can state your position while at the same time assuring him that you intend to obey him.

Merton thought Thompson's article might bear fruit in the wider context of race relations in the United States. Hopeful in Lyndon Johnson's presidency (1963–68), Merton continued,

> The way I look at it is this: the opportunity came, and you took it. You have spoken, knowing he might not like what you said, he is now angry, but you said what you felt was necessary. For

7. Thompson and Griffin, "Dialogue," 24–33.

8. Merton-Thompson correspondence, TMC. For Bishop Greco, see "Bishop Charles Pasquale Greco."

the moment, there is nothing more to do but simply to let the article have its effect. Your silence and other limitations at the moment will contribute to the force of the article. I hope it is all thoroughly investigated. But what President Johnson said about unity and avoiding hate certainly rings a bell.

Replying on December 5, 1963, Thompson thanked Merton and included a copy of his letter to Bishop Greco. Following Merton's counsel, Thompson professed his love for church and bishop. "If I have done harm to the Church, the Bishop or anyone else, I am truly sorry and beg forgiveness. I acted as I did in the past, only imprudently, yet only because I thought I had the permission to do so. I acted out of love and zeal for the Church." Thompson continued,

> I do think though that the whole thing is having a soul stirring effect on many. It is only because it is so true that many are uncomfortable. Many of the young priests at our day of recollection told me they appreciated it. A few of the older priests could not see his objection. I have a few priests and Sisters too who have written. One convent around New Orleans told me they are definitely sure they want a Negro Postulant now to start to ease their consciences. I hope they mean more than one however.

In another letter, dated February 20, 1964, Thompson wrote Merton about violence in his parish. Thompson mentioned five floggings and a chain letter from someone in Houston raising money for the mother of Medgar Evers (1925–63). Evers was an African American civil rights activist and NAACP field secretary in Mississippi killed by a Klansman.[9] Thompson also commented on the assassination of John F. Kennedy, whose presidency had sparked violence.

> Let me say that was a great shock to us here also the death of the President. Yet, great was & is the shock to see just how deep the hatred of Kennedy is. It is not an exaggeration that some kids shouted at hearing of his death, both in Dallas & Jackson & other places too I hear. Around here the expressions of joy & sorrow that his brother or wife did not get hit are common talk. We are the ones who have given these kids the idea of hate. What kind of ideas are they going to give their kids unless we do something about it now! God forgive us for our silence! How the words of Fr. Delp could be applied in our situation.

9. In February 1994, years after Evers's death, his murderer, Byron De La Beckwith, was convicted and sentenced to life in prison. Beckwith died in 2001 at the age of eighty.

Alfred Delp was a Jesuit priest falsely implicated in a failed plot to overthrow Hitler and executed on February 2, 1945. Delp's *Prison Meditations* were first published in German. In an introduction to the English translation Merton underscored the importance of Delp's legacy and called for respect and mutual respect and human solidarity among all races and nations.[10]

In his letter to Thompson, Merton acknowledged,

> I think we have to face the very serious fact that in the Church today "obedience" is invoked constantly to frustrate the real work that ought to be done for genuine issues (war, race, etc). The principles remain perfectly true: subject does lack information, perhaps cannot judge sufficiently well, etc but when the decision is constantly pushed back higher up and when no decision comes from higher up except to play safe and do nothing, there is a real problem . . . I guess I am really too much out of the picture to have anything to say. . . . I still find it hard to understand things like those floggings. I suppose there is no real way of understanding them.

Merton continued, commenting on the evil of violence unmasked by racial tensions of the day and by the assassination of President Kennedy. The illusion of the United States as a "nation of good people" particularly disturbed Merton, who urged Thompson to acknowledge violence in his own heart and to rely completely on God rather than his own strength.

> Such things are incredible in a country that makes the claims to civilization that ours does. The evil of violence is very deep in this land, and there is great sinfulness reaching down into the depths of this people, in spite of their pleasant exterior. It makes me very afraid to think of the consequences that will one day make themselves felt. The Kennedy affair was just one little symptom of this sin that is everywhere and that people don't seem to be able to take seriously. On the contrary, they are fed with it more and more. How can this nation have the illusion that it is a nation of good people? It makes you shudder. All I can say is that I certainly hope God will protect you and your people, and that something can be done to change things. You will need an awful lot of courage and trust, and that is why you must see to it as far as you can that there is as little as possible of the same violence in your own heart. The courage that is without violence is the greatest of all, because it relies completely on God and not on man's strength.

10. Merton, "Introduction," xxiv.

Earlier, Merton had published a book that year entitled *Praying the Psalms*. Believing the Psalms to be important for oppressed people, Merton had written that there is "no spiritual need of man that is not depicted and lived out in the Psalms."[11] Drawing on his monastic practice of prayer, Merton thought the Psalms contained real expression of the sufferings and conflicts that Thompson faced. In the face of such evil, Merton concluded by advising Thompson, "Fill your heart with the Psalms and Christ will live and fight in you." Promising to keep Thompson in his masses and prayers, Merton closed his lengthy letter, "Keep me posted. All best wishes."[12]

Merton's relationship with Thompson was one of friend and ally, roles that enabled Merton to respond compassionately to someone who experienced firsthand the pernicious effects of racism. In "The Black Revolution: Letters to a White Liberal," published in the issue of *Ramparts* that included Thompson's dialogue with John Howard Griffin, Merton saw African Americans as having spiritual insights that had to be taken seriously. He wrote of the voice of the American Negro as having "a genuine prophetic ring." Merton asked,

> Who knows if we will ever get another chance to hear it? In any case the Negro demands that his conditions be met with full attention and seriousness. The white man may not fully succeed in this—but he must at least try with all the earnestness at his command. Otherwise the moment of grace will pass without effect. The merciful *kairos* of truth will turn into the dark hour of destruction and hate. . . . And perhaps, somewhere, out of the ruins, a new world (a black world) will one day arise. . . . [is the] white man even capable of grasping the words, let alone believing them. For the rest, you have Moses and the Prophets: Martin Luther King, James Baldwin and others. Read them, and see for yourself what they are saying.[13]

Merton's exchange with Thompson occurred at a time of Merton's growing attention to the need for racism awareness work by whites and blacks alike. Merton's encouragement may have buoyed Thompson, whose ministry ultimately extended over a forty-three-year career. At the end of his life, in an interview on August 27, 1999, with David Prescott Talley (1950–), newly appointed bishop of the Alexandria, Louisiana diocese,

11. Merton, *Praying the Psalms*, 44.

12. Merton to Thompson, February 27, 1964. David Golemboski explores Merton's theological perspective on good and evil: "Mysterious, Unaccountable Mixture of Good and Evil," 88–101.

13. *Passion for Peace*, 187.

Thompson described himself as crazy enough to respond at age fifteen to a call to study for the priesthood. Recalling Ku Klux Klan activities in Louisiana, Thompson said that he never got scared. What surprised him was his ability to have fulfilled his calling to serve Christ faithfully as a black priest in a racist context.[14]

A second correspondent for whom Merton similarly played a role as ally and friend was a musician, Robert Lawrence Williams. Born in Louisville, Kentucky, Williams was, at the time of his exchange with Merton, a vocalist and President-Founder of the National Foundation for African Students in Boston, Massachusetts. The two men corresponded from 1964 to 1968. In his initial letter to Merton, Williams sought to commission Merton to write a series of poems on Faith and Brotherhood that he (Williams) would set to music and present in a concert in November 1964 as a tribute "to our late beloved friend, President John Kennedy." As well as providing a tribute to Kennedy," Williams wanted to offer "African and Negro youngsters a chance to educate themselves in such a way that they might in turn help in educating their people."[15]

Merton wrote eight "Freedom Songs."[16] Though he did not think highly of them,[17] he sent them to Williams who replied, thanking Merton for the "beautiful Freedom Songs."

> I especially love the last one, *Earthquake.* I had something like this one in mind when I wrote asking you for a patriotic number. This is truly a patriotic number, but not to the land and world we know, but to the New World, over which Our Lord Jesus shall rule. I like also the one "I Have Called You." I love them all and already my heart has begun to sing them, even though the music for them is still in heaven. I have started trying to get

14. AlexandriaDiocese, "Fr August Thompson Video."

15. "Merton's Correspondence with: Williams, Robert Lawrence," March 14, 1964.

16. The texts are in *Collected Poems of Thomas Merton* (1977). The titles and paging are as follows: "Sundown," 756–57; "Evening Prayer," 711–12; "All the Way Down," 669–70; "I Have Called You," 714–15; "Be My Defender," 692–93; "The Lord is Good," 775–76; "There Is a Way," 779–80; "Earthquake," 701–3. Merton wrote these poems in 1966, as well as other poems on racial justice such as "And the Children of Birmingham" (335–37). On Merton-Williams, Shannon's entry, "Freedom Songs," in *Thomas Merton Encyclopedia,* 167; Merton, *Hidden Ground of Love,* 587–607, includes some of Merton's letters to Williams, but not those by Williams to Merton.

17. In a September 18, 1965, journal entry, Merton called them "bad poems, written at the request of a young Negro singer for a fittingly idealistic project" (*Dancing in the Water of Life,* 325).

in touch with Aaron Copeland and feel in my heart already that God will inspire his heart to help us.[18]

A month later, Williams reported to Merton that Copeland wished them luck with the project, but that he could not then take on more work.[19] Later, the composer Alexander Peloquin agreed to write music for them.

During the exchanges between Williams, Merton, and Peloquin, misunderstandings arose over control of the project and copyright. At times, Williams charged that Merton and Peloquin, two white men, were continuing a tradition of racial exploitation. Tensions finally abated, and Merton arranged with Coretta Scott King for a tribute concert in memory of Martin Luther King Jr. On August 20, 1968, Peloquin conducted the score at the National Liturgical Conference in Washington, DC. The choir of Ebenezer Baptist Church in Atlanta, Dr. King's congregation, performed the concert along with members of Peloquin's choir.

On October 17, 1964, Williams wrote Merton that he desired to visit Gethsemani. I have found no evidence it took place, but Williams did thank Merton for sending Negro Digest [Jet], a Negro publication.

> Thank you Father Louis, for seeing God in black faces and hearts also; for loving us, and for caring about us. The more I read about you, the more I see that this wonderful love for our people was established in your heart by God, long before He lead you to Gethsemani. Thus I know you understand so well, the great fire that consumes my heart also.

In another letter dated October 27, 1964, Williams confirmed that the Freedom Songs were being translated into French. He opined that French-language readers would respond positively to the Freedom Songs and "love them as everyone does who has read them here."

> As you say, when it is God's time all will be well . . . in the meantime I will continue to study and perfect my talents and the foundation in preparation for the next work God is preparing us for. Father [his confessor] says there is a great need for young men like myself in both races today and he has a feeling . . . that I will do much good in the world. Please ask God, Father Louis, to give me more strength as well as patience. I do so very much want to use the talent he has given me for His Glory for I am aware that this is why He took my whole family, while I was a babe, and left only me.

18. Merton to Williams, June 9, 1964.
19. Merton to Williams, July 8, 1964.

In a letter dated December 21, 1964, Merton thanked Williams for getting the Freedom Songs translated into French. In his response to Williams, Merton tried to interpret why people feared the civil rights movement.

> You are right about the reactions of people, composers, who are on the lookout for money and prestige. It is true also that people are frightened of the civil rights cause. But that is no credit to them at all, and has nothing to do with the matter: except that of course anyone who is not committed would barely be able to do a good job in writing the music. Never mind, though, I can tell you from long experience that when God wills to bring fruit from a work, He makes it wait and puts all sorts of obstructions in the way, or lets them be put there, in order to really bring the thing to maturity. I am sure it will work this way. Do not worry, Freedom Songs will be needed for a long time to come, I am afraid.

Merton went on to comment on wider political events. Merton thought that Williams

> you are right about the Congo. This is another symptom of the same terrible blindness and confusion that is everywhere. People just do not seem to understand what is going on in Viet Nam, Africa, etc., etc. They are so used to fiction and TV drama that they can't understand the complexities of the truth. They think that the world is divided up into good guys and bad guys, and they make up their own minds as to which is which, and once they have decided that they are the good guys, everything else automatically falls into place. This country needs lots of prayers. It is terribly misguided on a lot of crucial issues.

Merton also mentioned an exhibition of his abstract drawings in Louisville. He expressed the hope that, if some of the paintings were sold, a scholarship could be established for an African girl to attend Catherine Spalding College, Louisville. Merton observed that such a scholarship for an African "would tie in with your [Williams'] project to some extent. We will see what the future brings."

Separately, Merton sent Williams a copy of his book *Seeds of Destruction*. Williams responded, thanking Merton and mentioning that he was to give a concert for the Franciscan Missionary Sisters of Africa on March 28, 1965. Williams promoted the book. When talking about it to the Franciscan Missionary Sisters, Mother Superior said, "I am reading *Seeds of Destruction* it now and I feel that it and the past Council will have much to do in getting our Catholic Friends on the ball. . . . God is so very good and I have always been aware of his loving hand upon my head. I desire only to be worthy of the work He has entrusted to me."[20]

In other exchanges with Williams, Merton offered a relationship of friend and ally much as he embraced with Father Thompson. Merton expressed concern in a manner that few if any whites could. In an apt phrasing, Williams affirmed that he saw Merton as "God's messenger, for only He could have revealed such things to you, when others with your same calling, also followers of The Lamb, have closed their hearts to The Lamb's gentle voice. I fear no longer for I see now that the same gentle voice speaks to us both and I too must obey, even as you already have."[21]

A third African-American with whom Merton interacted was the writer James Baldwin, author of *The Fire Next Time*, which closes with the dramatic line, "We can't ignore rainbow, fire next time."[22] The only known direct correspondence between the two men was a letter to Baldwin that Merton wrote shortly after having read *The Fire Next Time*. In it, Merton observed to Baldwin that human completeness comes only from the realization that "I am therefore not completely human until I have found myself in my African and Asian and Indonesian brother because he has the part of humanity which I lack."[23] In his journal, Merton commented,

> He [Baldwin] seems to know exactly what he is talking about, and his statements are terribly urgent. One of the things that makes most sense—an application of the ideas behind nonviolence, but I think it is absolutely true that the sit-in movement is not just to get the negroes a few hamburgers, it is for the sake of the white people, and for the country. He is one of the few genuinely concerned Americans, one whose concern I can really believe. The liberation of the Negroes is necessary for the liberation of the whites and for their recovery of a minimum of self-respect, and reality.[24]

Merton wrote Baldwin to express his sense of duty to try to make fellow whites to stop doing things they were doing with respect to racism.

20. Williams to Merton, January 15, 1965, folder #2 of 2, Merton-Williams 1966–1968 letters.

21. Williams to Merton, January 15, 1965.

22. Adapted from Baldwin, *Fire Next Time*, 106.

23. Merton, *Thomas Merton: A Life in Letters*, 226; also, Levrier-Jones, "Intriguing Lost Conversation of the Civil Rights Movement."

24. Merton, *Turning toward the World*, 297.

Merton indicated that he had to speak the truth about racism as he had come to understand the problem.[25]

Merton wrote several essays on racial justice, including "The Black Revolution: Letters to a White Liberal," mentioned earlier.[26] Two were book reviews. The first, "The Legend of Tucker Caliban" (1963), evaluated *A Different Drummer*, by William Melvin Kelley, who told the story of a black Southerner who one day salted his fields, burnt down his house, killed his livestock and, with his wife and child, set off a mass exodus of his mythical state's entire black population. In his review, Merton compared the book with Baldwin's *Fire Next Time*:

> It is the same message which the best American Negro writers are now, with a rather astonishing unanimity and confidence, announcing to the white world as their diagnosis of that world's sickness, with their suggestions for escaping the death which is otherwise inevitable. . . . These books tell us that it is the Negro who hears, or believes he hears, the true voice of God in history, and interprets it rightly. The white man has lost his power to hear any inner voice other than that of his own demon who urges him to preserve the *status quo* at any price, however desperate, however iniquitous and however cruel. The white man's readiness to destroy the world rather than change it is dictated by this inner demon, which he cannot recognize, but which the Negro clearly identifies.[27]

In an article entitled "The Meaning of Malcolm X," Merton reviewed *The Autobiography of Malcolm X*. After summarizing the early years of Malcolm Little (1925–65), Merton focused on Malcolm X's return from his 1964 pilgrimage to Mecca.

> Malcolm X first outgrew the ghetto underworld of prostitution, dope and crime. He then outgrew the religious underworld, the

25. Merton's letter to James Baldwin is in *Seeds of Destruction*, 306; for the wider Merton-Baldwin exchange, see Levrier-Jones, "Intriguing Lost Conversation of the Civil Rights Movement."

26. Paging for these essays is from Merton's *Passion for Peace*. Most appear in other publications. *The Literary Essays of Thomas Merton*, edited by the late Brother Patrick Hart (1981), includes "The Legend of Tucker Caliban" and reviews by Merton of works by Southern writers, notably William Faulkner and Flannery O'Connor, along with Merton's review of William Styron, *The Confessions of Nat Turner* (1967), and transcriptions of Merton's novice talks on Faulkner. Hart wrote of Merton's talk on Faulkner's *Sound and the Fury* as follows: "The words of Thomas Merton and William Faulkner speak eloquently for themselves in "the unburdening and the recollection of the Lamb." Merton, *Literary Essays*, 498.

27. Merton, *Passion for Peace*, 194–95.

spiritual power structure that thrives on a ghetto mystique. He was finally attaining to the freedom and fullness of understanding that gives some (still rare) American Negroes the sense of belonging to a world movement that makes them independent, to some extent, of purely American limitations and pressures. Malcolm grew too fast. He was too articulate. He was made to pay for it. The impact of his message to others that may follow him has only been made stronger and more emphatic by his death . . . . He was a fighter whose sincerity and courage we cannot help admiring, and who might have become a genuine revolutionary leader—with portentous effect in American society![28]

In Merton's 1967 essay, "The Hot Summer of Sixty-Seven," Merton observes that Malcolm X became a symbol of a black man who had fought his way free. Lamenting his death in 1965, Merton saw him as "a fearless and lucid black man who realized that no white man could be trusted."[29]

Merton's essay "From Non-Violence to Black Power" introduced section three of a book entitled *Faith and Violence: Christian Teaching and Christian Practice*. Merton opened by quoting "black power" leader H. Rap Brown: "Violence is as American as cherry pie."[30] Merton wrote, "There is a lot of truth in this arraignment of white America."[31] Merton acknowledged the need to embrace African-Americans in a manner that went beyond paternalism. Most significantly, Merton insisted on black agency: "We have to make a clear decision. Black Power or no Black Power, I for one remain *for* the Negro. I trust him, I recognize the overwhelming justice of his complaint, I confess I have no right whatever to get in his way, and that as a Christian, I owe him support, not in his ranks but in my own, among the whites who refuse to trust him or hear him, and who want to destroy him."[32]

"Religion and Race in the United States" originally appeared in a French publication in 1964, and in English in *New Blackfriars* in 1965. Merton argued that achieving civil rights legislation—again under threat—was the first phase of a wider process. Most importantly, Merton saw that such laws as the Civil Rights Act of 1964 and Voting Rights Act of 1965 failed to address systemic evil. Wounds were too deep to be cured by legislative advances alone.

28. Merton, *Passion for Peace*, 274–75. Merton's essay first appeared in the summer 1967 issue of *Continuum* and was reprinted widely. Random House first published *The Autobiography of Malcolm X* in 1964.

29. Merton, *Passion for Peace*, 291.

30. Merton, *Passion for Peace*, 210.

31. Merton, *Passion for Peace*, 212.

32. Merton, *Passion for Peace*, 216, emphasis in the original.

> The American racial crisis which grows more serious every day
> offers the American Christian a chance to face a reality about
> himself and recover his fidelity to Christian truth, not merely
> in institutional loyalties and doctrinal orthodoxies . . . but in
> recanting a more basic heresy: the loss of that Christian sense
> which sees every other man as Christ and treats him as Christ.[33]

Merton saw the need to confront racism at the heart of the very structures of white-dominated society. "The problem is to eradicate this basic
violence and injustice from white society. Can it be done? How?"[34]

In a novice talk given on June 10, 1964, Merton provided a partial
response to this query. Merton explained that problems like racism must
be "settled by people who are willing to seek justice and seek reconciliation
and unity on a higher plane and not just be seeking that our side's going
to win." Merton concluded, "we should be in this." Just as the Birmingham
campaign enabled "Negroes [to realize] that they're important [and] can
come out and do something and it mean something" monks can do "little
acts of service . . . for the world" like eschewing "violence of the tongue,"
meditating and maintaining spiritual health. "If a person is constantly
down and constantly griping and constantly with a long face . . . it's going
to be a drag on everybody."[35]

Merton lamented that unless the church took an active role in healing
divisions between black and white Americans, it would be among those
judged for its failure to address systemic racism. His conference ended
abruptly when the monastery bell rang. Nevertheless, he had provided
the novices a road map to guide them towards a more racially just world.
His insights mirrored a comment by an African American community
organizer with whom I worked in Berkeley, California during the summer
of 1964. Upon learning of the legislation, he said, "We've crossed a river.
There's a mountain ahead."

In a journal entry for September 10, 1965, Merton mentioned the visit
to Gethsemani of Baptist minister, activist, author, and lecturer Will Davis
Campbell (1924–2013).and James Young Holloway (1927–2002), at the
time Professor of Philosophy and Religion at Berea College in Kentucky and
editor of Katallagete, journal of the Committee of Southern Churchmen.
Merton wrote about their visit in his journal, as follows:

33. Merton, Passion for Peace, 226.

34. Merton, Passion for Peace, 227.

35. Merton, "Some Points from the Birmingham Non-violence Movement," 13–22.
The talk is also available in Houck and Dixon, Rhetoric, Religion, and the Civil Rights
Movement, 744–52.

There has been much more trouble (race riots) in many cities I had heard nothing about. Consciously or unconsciously I think the riots are in some sense being provoked by the police. Not as a deliberate plot, but as a self-fulfilling prophecy. Violence is so constantly expected that their tenseness, "aggressivity," and "brutality" provoke it in the end. And doubtless they feel so menaced that they think they are not being brutal at all.[36]

One outcome of the visit was the publication "The Hot Summer of 1967" in the Winter 1967–68 issue of *Katallagete*. The article proved to be Merton's final extensive discussion of the struggle for racial justice in the United States. Merton recalled that in his "Letters to a White Liberal," he was lifting up the efforts of Dr. Martin Luther King Jr. to solve the race problem by Christian nonviolence. At the time, Merton thought that this was "the *last chance* [his emphasis] to really do something by a peaceful revolution and that it was perhaps already too late." He maintained that the only possible solution was for everyone to pool their resources and to work together for a radical, creative change in social structures. "The only hope of peace and order would be, I think, the creation of a truly new and truly 'Great Society' in which the two races could share the same advantages not only on paper but in fact."[37]

A year later, Merton planned a retreat with Dr. King and the Buddhist monk Nhat Hanh at the Abbey of Gethsemani. All three practiced meditation for their spiritual fulfillment and that of others. Each sought to help others to live compassionately. One can only imagine how their dialogue might have ensued had Dr. King not been murdered after speaking in Memphis, Tennessee April 4, 1968. Merton heard of Dr. King's death while returning from a visit to a Shaker community in eastern Kentucky. In his journal, Merton wrote, "it [King's murder] lay on the top of the traveling car like an animal, a beast of the apocalypse. And it finally confirmed all the apprehensions—the feeling that 1968 is a beast of a year."[38]

36. Merton, *Dancing in the Water of Life*, 292. Merton wrote several articles published in *Katallagete*, including "Godless Christianity," in which he commented on the "death of God" movement of the 1960s. In exchanges with Campbell and Holloway, Merton exhibited a role of letter-writer and spiritual director. For example, in a January 15, 1968 letter, Merton encouraged Holloway to "keep Will Campbell's wife in your prayers and masses. She is to have an operation Tuesday." Merton to Holloway, Merton Correspondence Files, TMC.

37. See "The Hot Summer of 1967," in Merton, *Passion for Peace*, 287. Democratic President Lyndon B. Johnson sought to actualize his vision of the "Great Society" through legislation enacted by Congress in 1964–65.

38. Merton, *Other Side of the Mountain*, 78, entry for April 6, 1968. For an imagined account of the proposed retreat, see chapter 8.

Later, Merton sent Coretta Scott King a condolence letter through June Yungblut, the Atlanta-based Quaker who had helped organize the proposed retreat. In his journal, Merton copied words of Yungblut who had written, "And after that, maybe, the deluge."[39]

Reflecting on Merton's writings on racial justice while at the Merton archives during the summer of 2018, I asked Paul Pearson if he had any idea why Merton's important exchanges with Thompson, Williams, Baldwin, and Yungblut, as well as his essays on racial justice have been given less attention than his contributions on the Vietnam War, interfaith, or peace. Paul observed that the whole area of Merton on race seems to have been underdeveloped, a point he reiterated during the ITMS session at which I read this paper. Ever modest, he did not mention his essay on Merton's voice for racial justice.[40]

Nonetheless, the voice of Merton has recently received increasing attention. The TMC has compiled a list of secondary sources, recordings and African-American Correspondents. Materials are also available on the internet. For example Daniel P. Horan, OFM, assistant professor of systematic theology at Catholic Theological Union, spoke on the theme at St. Norbert College on November 2017. His talk is available online, under the title "Racism, White Privilege, and Thomas Merton on Transformative Spirituality and Justice."[41]

In the "authorized" biography of Merton, Michael Mott wrote that there were "serious flaws" in Merton's writings on racial questions. Mott observed that Merton was not alone among intellectuals "prone to attack" but who failed to offer solutions. Mott added that Merton provided "original and valuable insight" by moving beyond benevolence.[42]

Other authors have evaluated Merton's contribution on racial justice more positively. For example, Eldridge Cleaver, onetime Black Panther and candidate for the presidency of the United States on the Peace and Freedom Party ticket, wrote that he read Merton's *Seven Storey Mountain* while in prison. He recalled Merton's description of Harlem as especially haunting:

> Despite my rejection of Merton's theistic world view, I could not
> keep him out of the room. He shouldered his way through the

39. Merton, *Other Side of the Mountain*, 79, entry for April 6, 1968. For details on Merton's reaction to the assassination of Martin Luther King Jr., see Apel, "Crisis of Faith," 67–74.

40. Pearson, "Voice for Racial Justice," 46–47.

41. St. Norbert College, "'Racism, White Privilege, and Thomas Merton.'" The TMC houses tapes of twelve talks on "Thomas Merton for Our Time" can be found at www.NowYouKnowMedia.com.

42. Mott, *Seven Mountains of Thomas Merton*, 390.

door. Welcome, Brother Merton. I give him a bear hug. Most impressive of all to me was Merton's description of New York's black ghetto—Harlem. I liked it so much I copied out the heart of it in longhand . . . Whenever I felt myself softening, relaxing, I had only to read that passage to become once more a rigid flame of indignation.[43]

To celebrate Merton's contribution to racial justice, the TMC has had an annual Black History Month lecture. On February 22, 2010, Bryan N. Massingale, professor of theological and social ethics at Fordham University in New York City, spoke at Bellarmine University. In his talk, "Engaging Racism," Massingale asked, "What made it possible for Merton to speak out when others did not?"[44]

The present essay provides a partial answer to this question. From his university studies, the brief period in 1941 when he lived in Harlem and for twenty-seven years in the Deep South, especially during the turbulent 1960s, Merton reflected deeply on racial justice in friendships, through his novitiate conferences, in poetry and in several significant articles. For Merton, the search for racial justice was not merely a political issue. Rather, he saw racism as a profound spiritual crisis. Merton's radical anthropology and spirituality led him to discern the 1960s as a time of *kairos*, a classical Greek word meaning the right, critical, or opportune moment.

During the 1950s, Catholics tended to protest conscious acts of deliberate malice rather than to oppose systematic injustice. Merton was ahead of his time in analyzing the structures that sustained racism and, as a white living in the South, in acknowledging his duty, and the duty of all Christians to be open to discern truth in what Black Power advocates were saying.

Racism and racial strife remain palpable in the United States and worldwide. Many in the United States claim the country to be a Christian nation. In order to justify such a claim, people of faith must sustain a sincere connection between gospel values and the real needs of real people, including food, water, shelter, and freedom from racial attack.[45]

On October 27, 1964, in a letter to Robert Williams already referenced, Merton anticipated that his Freedom Songs and other writing on racial justice would continue to be needed for a long time. Writing Father Thompson, Merton shared having received a "hair-raising letter" from John

43. Cleaver, *Soul on Ice*, 34–35.

44. A tape of Dr. Massingale's lecture, "Engaging Racism," is available at TMC.

45. See Rohr, "Meditation: The Strength of the Link." Richard Rohr is a Franciscan who heads The Center for Action and Contemplation in Albuquerque, New Mexico. In his book *The Naked Now*, Rohr highlights Merton's insight that "We [humans] are too rational . . . all that is best is unconscious or superconscious." Rohr, *Naked Now*, 112.

Howard Griffin. Merton sensed the need for racial justice had deepened: "We are really on the verge of some earth shaking trouble which cannot be avoided or side stepped, and it is going to be very tragic for a lot of people (and probably not for those who need a little more tragedy in their lives, but for those who already have much more than they need). Now is the time when it is more necessary than ever to believe and to respond to one's fellow human beings in whatever predicament."[46]

The road ahead will not be easy. As a personal recollection, I recall the 1960 campaign when my Sunday school teacher in a Baptist congregation asked our class to fall on our knees and to pray that Kennedy, a Catholic, not be elected. Racism was also evident in Tennessee, where Republican Governor Bill Lee faced public backlash after he declared Saturday, July 13, 2019, Nathan Bedford Forrest Day. This continued a decades-old tradition honoring the Confederate general, slave trader, and onetime leader of the Ku Klux Klan.[47] Similar incidents elsewhere around the world led *New York Times* columnists Weiyi Cai and Simone Landon to write of "white extremism on the march." In their article, they exposed a vast global network spreading an ideology of hatred.[48]

As indicated through exchanges with three significant African American civil rights activists, Thomas Merton inspired worldwide a generation of readers and correspondents to work towards "a brotherhood of man."[49] Merton continues to inspire efforts to ensure that vision becomes a reality.

Fifty years after his death, Merton continues to provide a roadmap for people seeking to realize a Biblical vision that humans live with neither greed, nor hunger, nor anything that undermines full inclusivity and mutuality of everyone irrespective of religion or race. To paraphrase John Lennon's "Imagine," Merton was a dreamer, not the only one, who invited others to live at peace, one with another. As Merton wrote Robert Williams, let us work to ensure everyone claim their gifts and "have joy and hope in Christ, in whom all are one."[50]

46. Merton to Thompson, November 9, 1967.

47. Eckert, "Tennessee Governor Faces Backlash."

48. Cai and Landon, "Attacks by White Extremists Are Growing."

49. John Lennon, "Imagine."

50. Merton to Williams, May 27, 1965.

Section Two: **Loving Kindness**

Introduction

Be merciful, just as your Father is merciful.

—Luke 6:36

HEBREW SCRIPTURE AND THE Newer Testament refer to God as full of lovingkindness, compassion, and mercy. Translators have used these words interchangeably. The Hebrew carries the meaning "womb," suggesting God is loving, compassionate, and merciful like a mother.

In Luke 15:11–32, the story of the prodigal son, a father has two sons. The younger claims his inheritance. The father grants his son's request. This enables him to travel to a distant land, where he loses his fortune and returns home to face the consequences. To his surprise and in the face of his elder sibling's anger, the loving father welcomes the return of his son and throws an extravagant party. Envious, the older son refuses to participate. The father tells him, "Son, you are always with me, and all that is mine is yours. But we had to celebrate and rejoice, because this brother of yours was dead and has come to life; he was lost and has been found."

Nikos Kazantzakis (1883–1957) in *Report to Greco*, William Shakespeare (1564–1616) in *Henry IV Part II*, Anne Tyler (b. 1941) in *A Spool of Blue Thread*, and others have explored the story. Among songwriters, Kate Campbell (b. 1961) recorded "The Prodigal" on *Wandering Strange*.

In the sixties, Merton was reading the Bohemian-Austrian poet-novelist Rainer Maria Rilke (1875–1926). Merton mentioned Rilke's *New Poems* (2007; German: *Neue Gedichte*), *Duino Elegies* (1923), and "Olive Garden." Reflecting on "the agony of Gethsemani," Merton wondered, "Catholics have probably read with severe displeasure as a denial of faith.

Is it, though?" Merton thought not and found the different moods and intonations of Rilke "lovely and funny."[1]

In an essay entitled "The Prodigal Son," Rilke focused characterized story as a legend of a man who did not want to be loved. As a "slowly recovering convalescent," he almost forgot God in the difficult work of approaching him, and all that he hoped to perhaps attain with him in time was "*sa patience de supporter une âme*" ("his patience to support a soul"). The wayward brother ultimately had a great transformation: "Love. My God, it is love."[2]

Another writer, Henri J. M. Nouwen (1932–96), explored how seeing a reproduction of Rembrandt's prodigal son painting led him to identify with each person in the story: the wayward younger brother, the resentful older brother, and the compassionate father. Nouwen briefly met Merton at Gethsemani. In an interview, he described the occasion as ordinary, yet revelatory of Merton's compassion.[3]

Campbell, Rilke, Nouwen, and Merton all highlight the thread of lovingkindness woven throughout Merton's writings. The first article in this section, "The Wilderness of Compassion," originated as a paper read at the 15th general ITMS meeting in June 2017 at St. Bonaventure University, Olean, New York. I wrote the second, "Ishi, Messenger of Hope," for *We Are Already One: Thomas Merton's Message of Hope; Reflections to Honor His Centenary (1915–2015)*, edited by Gray Henry and Jonathan Montaldo (Louisville: Fons Vitae, 2014).

---

1. Merton, *Dancing in the Water of Life*, 316, entry for November 15, 1965.

2. See "The Prodigal Son" in Rilke, *Ahead of All Parting*, 276, my translation.

3. Nouwen, *Return of the Prodigal Son*; for Nouwen's appreciation of Merton, see Bob Grip, "Henri Nouwen on Thomas Merton."

3

Wilderness of Compassion

ON JUNE 13, 1951, Merton wrote in his journal that he sat on "the threshold of a new existence." Merton observed, "The one who is going to be most fully formed by the new scholasticate is the Master of Scholastics. It is as if I were beginning all over again to be a Cistercian. . . . The only essential is . . . God Himself."[1]

What prompted Merton to believe he was becoming a monk different than the one who had already spent a decade at Gethsemani? Biographer Michael Mott suggested Merton was experiencing a "stability crisis" engendered in part by the popularity of *The Seven Storey Mountain* and *The Sign of Jonas*.[2] William H. Shannon, ITMS founder, general editor of the Thomas Merton letters, and coeditor (with Christine M. Bochen and Patrick F. O'Connell) of *The Thomas Merton Encyclopedia*, proposed that what was going on in Merton "was the maturing realization, born of this contemplation, that it is not possible to leave the world in any real sense . . . There is simply no place else to go . . . The experience challenged the concept of a separate 'holy' existence lived in a monastery. He experienced the glorious destiny that comes simply from being a human person and from being united with, not separated from, the rest."[3]

For Merton, the human/divine contrast was altogether crucial. As a man alive within a world the Holy One created and sustained, Merton understood he was a person like any other, an ordinary mortal on earth. Merton knew he was no saint but was transformed having been birthed in the image and likeness of God.

---

1. Merton, *Entering the Silence*, 460.
2. Mott, *Seven Mountais of Thomas Merton*, 273.
3. Quoted in Erickson, "Thomas Merton's Mystical Vision in Louisville," para. 4.

On March 3, 1951, Merton journaled that he welcomed his new assignment as Master of Scholastics as an opportunity to "live as a member of the human race."[4] Merton acknowledged that he may have entered the Abbey of Gethsemani not simply to flee the world—he had just been drafted for military service in World War II—but to find his place in the world.[5] A decade later, he understood his monastic vocation more positively:

> My first duty is to start, for the first time, to live as a member
> of the human race, which is no more (and no less) ridiculous
> than I am myself. And my first human act is the recognition of
> how much I owe to everybody else. . . . But the world also was
> made by God and is good, and, unless that world is our mother,
> we cannot be saints, because we cannot be saints unless we are
> first of all human.[6]

Certain of God's creative and dynamic intervention in his life, Merton understood that the contemplative life was true not simply for monks and nuns, but for everyone. By seeking to be fully active, alive, awake, and aware, each and every person can know God as God really is and, knowing God, can recognize God at the core of his or her being. Merton described this as discovering one's "true self," a state of being with God in perfect freedom, love, and unity.

In *What Is Contemplation?* (1948) Merton wrote, "The seeds of this perfect life [contemplation] are planted in every Christian soul at Baptism. But seeds must grow and develop before you reap the harvest." Merton expressed concern about a Christian philosophy known as Quietism, a form of mysticism that insists on passivity as a condition of perfection. Proscribed as heretical during the seventeenth century, quietists, as described by Merton, were people who are "empty . . . of all love and all knowledge and remain inert in a kind of spiritual vacuum." In contrast with such selfishness, Merton encouraged "pure contemplatives let go of everything and, trusting God, allow the brightness of Jesus to shine in their lives."[7]

Writing in his journal three years later, Merton observed that his first months as Master of the Scholastics were a time when he had looked into the hearts of younger monks, taken on their burdens, and stumbled a lot. Discovering "the kind of work I once feared because I thought it would interfere with 'solitude' is, in fact, the only true path to solitude, Merton concluded, "Everything that affects you builds you into a hermit, as long as

---

4. Merton, *Entering the Silence*, 451.

5. Merton, *Bread in the Wilderness*, 11.

6. Merton, *Entering the Silence*, 451.

7. Merton, *What Is Contemplation?*, 17, 71–77.

you do not insist on doing the work yourself and building your own kind of hermitage." He asked,

> What is my new desert? The name of it is compassion. There is no wilderness so terrible, so beautiful, so arid and so fruitful as the wilderness of compassion. It is the only desert that shall truly flourish like the lily. It shall become a pool, it shall bud forth and blossom and rejoice with joy. It is the desert of compassion that the thirsty land turns into springs of water, that the poor possess all things. There are no bounds to contain the inhabitants of this solitude in which I live alone, as isolated as the Host on the alter, the food of all men, belonging to all and belonging to none, for God is with me, and He sits in the ruins of my heart, searching His Gospel to the poor.[8]

Several years later, in 1958, Merton found himself in Louisville at the corner of Fourth and Walnut, a busy downtown intersection. Merton awoke to his love of people and wrote of this moment in an oft-quoted passage of *Conjectures of a Guilty Bystander*:

> I was suddenly overwhelmed with the realization that I loved all those people, that they were mine and I theirs, that we could not be alien to one another even though we were total strangers. It was like waking from a dream of separateness, of spurious self-isolation in a special world, the world of renunciation and supposed holiness. The whole illusion of a separate holy existence is a dream.

Continuing his meditation, Merton wrote,

> I have the immense joy of being *man*, a member of a race in which God Himself became incarnate. As if the sorrows and stupidities of the human condition could overwhelm me, now I realize what we all are. And if only everybody could realize this! But it cannot be explained. There is no way of telling people that they are all walking around shining like the sun.[9]

Merton did not come easily to this self-understanding. He characterized his journey through a "wilderness of compassion" as a struggle, a prelude to something he could not have anticipated. Merton may have hoped that love and trust would triumph over fear and hatred, that people could work together to forge a world of peace with justice. He had grown

8. Merton, *Sign of Jonas*, 323, Merton's emphasis. Another Merton scholar, Mike Brennan, considers this theme in his "Walking with Thomas Merton," 321.

9. Merton, *Conjectures of a Guilty Bystander*, 156–57.

to realize that such dreams do not materialize, at least not for most of us, without a deep spirituality.

As early as his student years at Oakham, Merton supported the nonviolent *Satyagraha* (truth-force) that marked Gandhi's efforts to lead India to independence. Merton continued to decry violence and entered the monastery in part as an act of resistance to the Second World War.[10] At the time Merton wrote of his wilderness of compassion, the United States was at war in Korea. Merton felt called to protest such inhumanity. Although ordered, years later, not to write on such issues, he did not cease to brood about war. How could he not? After all, Strategic Air Command planes flew over his valley daily at 3:30 a.m. "loaded with strong medicine. Very strong. Strong enough to burn up all these woods and stretch our hours of fun into eternities."[11]

The wilderness of compassion theme pervaded Merton's prodigious literary output. For example, in *Bread in the Wilderness*, initially published in *Orate Fratres* in 1950, Merton explored the liturgical prayer of the monk as "one of the great pacifying influences in a life that is all devoted to serenity and interior peace." In a chapter entitled "The Shadow of Thy Wings," with a section on "The Silence of the Psalms." Merton focused on descriptions by the Psalmist of times of trouble, suffering, misery, darkness, or undertow. Yet Merton concluded that the Psalms "contain within themselves the silence of high mountains and the silence of heaven . . . when Christ must still perforce travel among us as a pilgrim disguised in our own tattered garments."[12]

In *The Wisdom of the Desert*, Merton identified with the early Christian hermits who abandoned the cities of late antiquity to live in solitude in the deserts of Egypt, Palestine, Arabia, and Persia. Asking why they did this, Merton summarized in one word, "salvation."[13] Yet even as monks fled to the desert to find the Holy during a time of the falling apart of things—characterized by historian Peter Brown as "confusing . . . a minefield with the snares of the devil"—they created a structure that "quite surpassed any of the organizational ventures of the late Roman state."[14]

In his role as Master of Scholastics (1951–55), and subsequently as novice master (1955–65), Merton gave conferences on the monastic

10. Jim Forest introduces Merton's application for conscientious objector status in *Merton Annual* 28 (2015) 25–29.

11. See "Rain and the Rhinoceros" in Merton, *Raids on the Unspeakable*, 14.

12. Merton, *Bread in the Wilderness*, 3, 129. See Bochen, "Bread in the Wilderness," 32–33.

13. Merton, *Wisdom of the Desert*, 3.

14. Brown, *World of Late Antiquity AD 150–750*, 99; Brown, "Rise and Function of the Holy Man in Late Antiquity."

tradition. Patrick F. O'Connell has transcribed and published many lectures in which we discern Merton's focus on compassion.

> The soul united to God in perfect love has no more anger, and hence does not judge sinners but has only compassion for them.[15]
>
> Heads of monasteries . . . are to have St. Paul's zeal and compassion . . . and to realize that in saving the souls of his monks he is saving his own soul.[16]
>
> Psalm 50 [51] is the fourth of the penitential psalms . . . *the psalm par excellence of Christian compunction. . . . God's pardon is not merely exterior, but it brings with it an interior transformation . . .* [God] looks upon us with fatherly compassion . . . the Spirit of His love takes over and rules our lives. He thus becomes the shepherd of our souls again. Then we taste the joy of His salvation.[17]

The Merton Seasonal recently published "In the Wilderness."[18] Merton originally wrote the essay for *No Man Is an Island*. Merton characterized wilderness, a word synonymous with desert, as a locale of alone-ness and physical solitude. Wilderness can be either a place of danger, suffering, darkness, poverty, and frustration, or an earthly paradise. By the early 1950s, Merton discovered his "wilderness of compassion" allowed him to remain alone. He understood this as an opportunity to do more good for the human race than was possible when he was "in the world," a prisoner of society.

For Merton, life at times seemed precarious. No more or less than anyone, monks worried. "There are times when he cannot think, except to think that he is probably going crazy."[19] Merton found an antidote to his dis-ease with the ways of the world by an interior solitude which can be had without physical isolation.

As Merton entered his second decade in the monastery, his journey inward deepened. His abbot granted him permission to spend periods of time at an old woodshed Merton dedicated to St. Anne, mother of Jesus' mother Mary. When he was there, with a view of cornfields and hills in the distance, there was "always lots of sky and lots of peace, and [he didn't] have distractions apart from obstreperous rats."[20] A place of silence and

15. Merton, *Cassian and the Fathers*, 113.

16. Merton, *Pre-Benedictine Monasticism*, 118.

17. Merton, *Monastic Observances*, 96–97, emphasis in original.

18. Merton, "In the Wilderness," 5–7.

19. Merton, "In the Wilderness," 6–7.

20. Merton, *Search for Solitude*, 29, entry for February 9, 1953. Nothing is known about the parents of the Virgin Mary, Joachim and Ann.

stillness, the shack met Merton's need for greater solitude. Paradoxically, periods at St Anne's prepared Merton to play a significant role beyond the monastery and Catholic Church.

On February 21, 1965, Merton advised friend Jim Forest to free himself from domination by causes, however just, and to live into Christ, trusting God go make something good from situations we cannot necessarily know all about beforehand. He later described this role in words that I quoted in the paper I prepared in 1971 for a meeting of the Monroe Baptist Association of the American Baptist Convention which was to assess my readiness for ordination into ministry.

> To turn to such a world, in which every other voice but the voice of God is heard and merely to add one more voice to the general din—one's own—is to neglect the ominous reality of a crisis that has perhaps become apocalyptic. In "turning to" this kind of world, I think the Catholic Church intends to respect the gravity of its predicament, and to do a little listening. There is certainly an enormous difference between the solemn anathemas of Vatican I and the more temperate and sympathetic appeals of Vatican II for dialogue. . . .
>
> My own peculiar task in my Church and in my world has been that of the solitary explorer who, instead of jumping on all the latest bandwagons at once, is bound to search the existential depths of faith in its silences, its ambiguities, and in those certainties which lie deeper than the bottom of anxiety. In these depths there are no easy answers, no pat solutions to anything. It is a kind of submarine life in which faith sometimes mysteriously takes on the aspect of doubt. When, in fact, one has to doubt and reject conventional and superstitious surrogates that have taken the place of faith. . . .
>
> On this level, the division between Believers and Unbeliever and others ceases to be so crystal clear. It is not that some are all right and others are all wrong: *all* are bound to seek in honest perplexity. Everyone is an Unbeliever more or less! Only when this fact is fully experienced, accepted and lived with, does one become fit to hear the simple message of the Gospel—or any other religious teaching.[21]

In discussion that followed, I emphasized that by responding to a call to ministry, I identified with Merton, who had (like myself, in the Russian Orthodox tradition) been baptized as an infant, came to faith as a young adult yet continued to struggle with authentic sincerity and openness, and

---

21. See "Apologies to an Unbeliever" in Merton, *Faith and Violence*, 212–13, emphasis in original. Grundmann's anthology, *Interreligious Dialogue*, reviewed in section 4.

who sought to follow Christ with humility, faith, and love to a society that in many ways had become post-Christian.

The gathering recommended my ordination despite a cautionary word by a gentleman who wondered if I was not too liberal and too ecumenical. In retrospect, like Merton, my faith has not exempted me from confronting serious questions raised by this well-intentioned brother, or doubts arising from evils such as the Holocaust, in which my great Aunt Leah Burstein died, or systemic racism that I have witnessed throughout my life. Just as Merton's "apology to an unbeliever" spoke to me in 1971, Merton's writings continue to encourage me and countless others to make God known to the stranger, the naked, the hungry, the thirsty, the sick, and the imprisoned who are ever in our midst (Matt 25:31–46).

Having concluded my ordination paper with this text, I have continued to identify with Merton whose "apology" remains as relevant today as in the 1960s. One reason is that church and society are both in crisis. Writing a "Dear Grandkids" article for the July 2017 issue of the *United Church Observer*, the Canadian novelist Margaret Atwood raises questions we do well to ponder: Why am I on the planet? What is a "good" life? What are my responsibilities for my fellow human beings? Atwood warns, "at this moment, we human beings are truly walking along the razor's edge."

While Atwood focuses on the bigger picture, many church people, faced with empty pews and diminished income, have come to the decision, sometimes very painful, to close or merge their congregation with others. The headline in a front-page story in *The Hamilton Spectator* for April 11, 2017 reads, "Final Service: Mount Hope United [Church of Canada] is Leaving the Village." Author Paul Wilson quotes pastor Ann Stafford as saying, "This is not a death. Or if it is, there's a resurrection after."

In this case, a hundred-year-old sanctuary serves as a place of worship for another spiritual community. In other cases, declining membership has generated renewal efforts. In the late 1980s, I helped establish at McMaster Divinity College a Center for Mission and Evangelism. My colleagues and I brought together core leaders from around the country—students and lay people—to participate in workshops, to rethink mission and evangelism, and to revalorize the role of institutional religion in contemporary society. We discovered that, on balance, scientific rationalism and technology had contributed to eco-destruction and human fragmentation. In response, we sought to nurture spiritual values that could prove attractive for the next generation and possibly contribute to renewal and growth.

In addition to Merton, a key model for me has been the Lutheran theologian Dietrich Bonhoeffer (1906–45), who, during the 1930s, helped form a Confessing Church movement in Germany to oppose Hitler. On January 14, 1935, Bonhoeffer wrote his brother Karl-Friedrich,

I think I am right in saying that I would only achieve true inner clarity and honesty by really starting to take the Sermon on the Mount seriously. Here alone lies the force that can blow all this idiocy sky-high—like fireworks, leaving only a few burnt-out shells behind. The restoration of the church must surely depend on a new kind of monasticism, which has nothing in common with the old but a life of uncompromising discipleship, following Christ according to the Sermon on the Mount.

More recently, the publishers of this book have encouraged a movement known as "the new monasticism," through its "new monastic library," described by author and series editor Jonathan Wilson-Hartgrove as follows:

> For over a millennium, if Christians wanted to read theology, practice Christian spirituality, or study the Bible, they went to the monastery to do so. There, people who inhabited the tradition and prayed the prayers of the church also copied manuscripts and offered fresh reflections about living the gospel in a new era. Two thousand years after the birth of the church, a new monastic movement is stirring in North America. In keeping with ancient tradition, new monastics study the classics of Christian reflection and are beginning to offer some reflections for a new era.[22]

My partner Nancy and I are members of the "Greater Community" of an innovative example of the new monasticism, Community of the Transfiguration in Australia.[23]

A final parallel concerns contemporary expressions of nationalism and dissent. I am concerned about anti-Judaism, anti-Islam, and, more generally, political expressions of paranoia and racism that continue to be manifest in the twenty-first century, notably in the United States, Brazil, and some European countries. In offering this reflection on loving-kindness in Merton, I trust readers might be moved from the hesitancies and soul-searching engendered by a number of concurrent crises—notably pandemic, racism, and hyper-nationalism—to help give birth to a new world of justice, loving-kindness, humility, and embrace of diversity envisioned by Merton.

22. See the series page at https://web.archive.org/web/20170624005647/https://wipfandstock.com/catalog/series/view/id/36/. Autographing a copy of his book *New Monasticism: What It Has to Say to Today's Church*, Jonathan Wilson-Hartgrove wrote, "For Paul, grateful to be with you on the Way."

23. Dekar, *Community of the Transfiguration*, and Metaxas, *Bonhoeffer: Pastor, Martyr, Prophet, Spy*, highlight Bonhoeffer's call for a new monasticism.

4

Ishi, Messenger of Hope

MERTON TOOK A SPECIAL interest in the ancient wisdom of Eastern religions, especially Buddhism. Merton believed he could also learn from the traditions of first peoples, including Inca and Mayan cultures overwhelmed by the Spanish conquest. Merton observed, "neither the ancient wisdoms nor the modern sciences are complete in themselves. They do not stand alone. They call for one another."[1] He also discerned, "Our task now is to learn that if we can voyage to the ends of the earth and there find ourselves in the aborigine who most differs from ourselves, we will have made a fruitful pilgrimage."[2]

After reading *Ishi in Two Worlds: A Biography of the Last Wild Indians in North America*, by Theodora Kroeber, Merton wrote a piece entitled "Ishi: A Meditation." The article was first published in the March 1967 issue of *The Catholic Worker*. Subsequently, it was included along with four others in *Ishi Means Man*. The collection reflects Merton's concern for not only the first inhabitants of North Americas but also the cargo-cult phenomenon described to him by Matthew Kelty.

Ishi (c. 1860–March 25, 1916) was the last known Yahi-Yana who lived in the foothills around present-day Lassen National Peak in California. In 1911, alone and starving, Ishi left his ancestral homeland. He spent his last five years in San Francisco as research subject and assistant for University of California anthropologists Alfred and Theodora Kroeber.

In the Yahi-Yana culture, it was rude to ask someone's name. When asked his name, Ishi said, "I have none, because there were no people to name me." Ishi meant that no Yahi-Yana had ever spoken his name. The Kroebers named him Ishi, meaning "man." Merton praised "loving kindness" lavished

1. Merton, *Gandhi on Non-Violence*, 1.
2. Merton, *Mystics and Zen Masters*, 112.

on Ishi by the Kroebers but lamented that Ishi's people had been "barbarously, pointlessly destroyed."[3]

Merton remonstrated against what he perceived to be a grave problem of institutional religion. He condemned "the almost total lack of protest on the part of religious people and clergy in the face of enormous social evils."[4] Writing in the context of the growing violence against people of color—Vietnamese, African Americans, and America's first people—Merton considered the treatment of Ishi as an extension of a frontier mentality, replete with enemies who were of an "inferior race." For Merton, the death of Ishi and extinction of his people were extreme examples of the capacity of technology potentially to eliminate entire tribes and ethnic groups, which Merton characterized as genocide.

> "Genocide" is a new word. Perhaps the word is new because technology has now got into the game of destroying whole races at once. The destruction of races is not new—just easier. Nor is it a specialty of totalitarian regimes. We have forgotten that a century ago white America was engaged in the destruction of entire tribes and ethnic groups of Indians. The trauma of California gold.[5]

Merton praised Theodora Kroeber's role in having saved Ishi and her writing about him with "impeccable objectivity" and "compassion." Merton wrote, "To read this story thoughtfully, to open one's ear to it, is to receive a most significant message: one that not only moves, but disturbs. . . . Unfortunately, we learned little or nothing about ourselves from the Indian wars."[6]

Merton condemned his own country with its incomparable technological power, its unequalled material strength, its psychic turmoil, its moral confusion, and its profound heritage of guilt. He condemned equally the pious declarations of the Catholic hierarchy, and the moral indifference of so-called realists who did nothing to change the situation.

> For the reflective reader who is—as everyone must be today—deeply concerned about man and his fate, this is a moving and significant book, one of those unusually suggestive works that *must* be read, and perhaps more than once.[7]

3. See "Ishi: A Meditation" in Merton, *Passion for Peace*, 265.

4. Merton, *Passion for Peace*, 127, review under a pseudonym, Benedict Monk, of *The Christian Failure*, by Ignace Lepp.

5. See "Ishi: A Meditation" in Merton, *Passion for Peace*, 263.

6. See "Ishi: A Meditation" in Merton, *Passion for Peace*, 264.

7. See "Ishi: A Meditation" in Merton, *Passion for Peace*, 268, Merton's emphasis.

Merton believed that much can be learned from traditional people like Ishi about community, ritual, and the spirit world. He saw the story of Ishi as a prologue to United States involvement in Vietnam. "What is most significant is that Vietnam seems to have become an extension of our old western frontier, complete with enemies of another 'inferior' race. This is a real 'new frontier' that enables us to continue the cowboys-and-Indians game which seems to be part and parcel of the national identity. What a pity that so many innocent people have to pay with their lives for our obsessive fantasies."[8] Merton decried the killing of innocent women and children. "In the end, it is the civilians that are killed in the ordinary course of events, and combatants only get killed by accident. No one worries any more about double effect. War is waged against the innocents to 'break enemy morale.'"[9]

In her forward to *Ishi Means Man*, Dorothy Day wrote that, after reading the essays in the book, she could only cry out, as did another staff member, "More, more." She continued,

> One feels a great sense of guilt at knowing so little about the Indians of the Americas. As children, when we played the game of Indians and cowboys, it was always the Indians who were the aggressors, the villains. And then in my late teens I read an account of the Jesuits among the Indians in upper New York state and in Canada, and remembered only the tortures undergone by the missionaries. . . . We quite forgot the story of our earliest colonists and the aid the Indians had given them, teaching them how to survive in what was, to them, a harsh and barren land, during those first winters.[10]

Born and raised in California, I was part of a generation that, in fourth grade, built models of church missions out of poster board to celebrate the role in the late 1700s of the Franciscan missionary Junípero Serra in establishing missions along the West Coast, including Mission Santa Clara, which hosted the general ITMS meeting in 2019.[11]

---

8. See "Ishi: A Meditation" in Merton, *Passion for Peace*, 269.

9. See "Ishi: A Meditation" in Merton, *Passion for Peace*, 269.

10. Day, *Ishi Means Man*, vii.

11. There is a statue of Father Serra, who in 1777 founded the mission. Nearby, and especially moving to me, were the memorial crosses recalling the Jesuit martyrs in El Salvador: Ignacio Ellacuría Beascoechea, SJ, the rector of the university; Ignacio Martín-Baró, SJ, vice-rector of the university and a leading expert on Salvadoran public opinion; Segundo Montes, SJ, dean of the department of social sciences; Juan Ramón Moreno, SJ; Joaquín López y López, SJ; Amando López, SJ; Elba Ramos, their housekeeper; and Celina Ramos, her sixteen-year-old daughter.

On Sunday afternoon outings, my family and I enjoyed visiting many of the beautiful buildings that are now historic landmarks. Only during my undergraduate work at the Berkeley campus of the University of California, where I enrolled in several anthropology courses, did I begin to understand the role of the church in a less benevolent light. This led to controversy in 2015, when, during his first visit to the United States, Pope Francis named Junípero Serra a saint.[12]

During the summer of 1965, I worked in Lassen Volcanic National Park in Northern California with a grassroots, student-led ministry, A Christian Ministry in the National Parks. The organization began in 1951 with the dream of providing Christian community for the people working in, living in, and visiting national parks. Reading local history, I learned of Ishi's fate and the extinction of the native population of the area.

The tragic story of Ishi culminated in 2000. After a long legal battle, a jar of "medical solution" containing the preserved brain of Ishi was removed from a shelf at the Smithsonian Institute and returned to a related tribe, the Pit River, for appropriate burial.[13]

There are many parallels of Merton's account of Ishi in the history of settler treatment of the indigenous populations of Canada and Australia. Settlers from Europe brought diseases that decimated indigenous communities. One unexpected consequence was the need to encourage immigration to work in the new settler colonies.

In Australia, England transported prisoners to work due to the absence of sufficient survivors among the indigenous population. In 1830, George Arthur, governor of the state of Tasmania, drew a line across the island to demark that part in which no aboriginal person could live. A woman named Truganini (c. 1812–May 8, 1876) was among those displaced. According to historian Henry Reynolds, a descendant of Tasmanian aboriginal people, settlers treated her death as an event of great significance and denunciation. Like Merton, Reynolds regarded the fate of Tasmanian aborigines as a chapter in the history of genocide.[14] Similarly, in *Brave New World*, Aldous Huxley warned that what was done to Truganini could be the fate of any population.

We live at a time of climate catastrophe, the destruction of the Amazonian rainforests, and the melting of Greenland's glaciers and of Arctic and Antarctic ice caps. There are some signs of hope. Social movements

12. For controversy surrounding the sainthood of Junípero Serra, the Franciscan missionary who founded nine missions, see Holson, "Sainthood of Junípero Serra Reopens Wounds."

13. Cienski, "Remains of Last Member of California Tribe."

14. Reynolds, *Why Weren't We Told?*, 13.

such as 350.org and the United Nations Framework Convention on Climate Change have generated activism by many citizens around the world who are concerned for our common future.

In 1998, during a sabbatical in Australia, I visited Tasmania, where I learned of protests that led to a blockade of efforts to build dams on the Franklin and Gordon rivers and, ultimately, cancellation of the project.[15] Five principles of the movement have shaped my understanding of a way to honor the legacy of Ishi, Truganini, and the "wisdom of the elders," title of a book by Canadian environmentalists David Suzuki and Peter Knudtson. The first principle is that earth has values for humankind that no scientist can synthesize, no economist can price, and no technological distraction can replace. The second principle is interconnection. All things are connected. What we do to the Earth, we do to ourselves. The third principle is the indivisibility of ecological justice, social justice, and peace. The fourth principle is the custodianship of the earth. The fifth principle is resistance.

These principles shape an earth first ethic. We should protect in perpetuity wild places, not only for our own sake, but for the sake of the plants, animals, and earth itself. In particular, we must let some wilderness areas exist intact solely for its own sake; no human justificaton, rationale, or excuse is needed. However challenging it may be to prioritize concern for our fellows and all creation, we must respect both past generations who lived closer to nature, and current or future generations that are more urban. Especially challenging is to balance our need for resources upon which we depend to live with respect for wild and scenic places and for those like Ishi who have cared for earth over the centuries.

15. Wilderness Society, *Franklin Blockade.*

Section Three: **Walking Humbly**

Introduction

THE CHAPTERS IN THIS section, and the book as a whole, present Merton's dream of a new world filled with justice-seeking, kind, and humble people. The word humble derives from the Latin *humus*, the black soil resulting from the partial decomposition of plant or animal matter. Humble people remind me of humus in three respects. First, they are not pie-in-the-sky dreamers but architects of a better common future as John Lennon sang in "Imagine": "A brotherhood of man . . . Imagine all the people sharing all the world."[1] In his April 4, 1967 speech, "Beyond Vietnam," Dr. Martin Luther King Jr. called for "a revolution of values" that would honor humility.[2] Second, humble people are deeply rooted. Just as humus works beneath the surface, the actions of humble people become intertwined with everything around them. Third, humble people draw from a source of life beyond themselves.

Merton considered humility a key value in his vocation. In talks on the Rule of Saint Benedict, he spoke of humility and obedience as key Benedictine practices. Merton deemed chapter 7, on humility, longest and most important, "for while all the rest more or less stresses the exterior conduct of the monk . . . *here we have for St. Benedict the real interior life of the monk.*"[3] In a chapter on "being and doing" in *No Man Is an Island*, Merton wrote, "The value of our activity depends almost entirely on the humility to accept ourselves as we are . . . . The fruitfulness of our life depends in large measure on our ability to doubt our own words and to question the value of our own

---

1. Lennon, "Imagine."
2. King, "Beyond Vietnam," 158.
3. Merton, *Rule of Saint Benedict*, 152, Merton's emphasis.

work."[4] In a chapter entitled "Humility against Despair" in *New Seeds of Contemplation*, Merton wrote,

> It is almost impossible to overestimate the value of true humility and its power in the spiritual life. For the beginning of humility is the beginning of blessedness and the consummation of humility is the perfection of all joy. Humility contains in itself the answer to all the great problems of the life of the soul. It is the only key to faith . . . for faith and humility are inseparable. In perfect humility all selfishness disappears and your soul is no longer lives for itself or in itself for God. And it is lost and submerged in Him and transformed into Him . . . and swims in the attributes of God, Whose power, magnificence, greatness and eternity have, through love, through humility become our own.[5]

For Merton, we cannot journey to paradise restored without walking humbly. In this section, I include three articles. The first, "The Power of Silence," appeared initially in *Fellowship*, the journal of the Fellowship of Reconciliation, an organization that facilitated Merton's meeting the Vietnamese monk, poet, and peacemaker Nhat Hanh on May 28, 1966.[6] Impressed, Merton wrote "Nhat Hanh Is My Brother," included in *Passion for Peace: The Social Essays*. We revisit Nhat Hanh in chapter 8.

The second, "Silence as Attention and Antidote," was published in *The Merton Seasonal* 40 (2015) 16–18. The third, "Divinization in Merton," originated as a paper read in 2013 at Sacred Heart University, Fairfield, Connecticut, host of the 13th ITMS general meeting. The theme of divinization or deification recurred throughout Merton's writing, notably in *The New Man* and in his novice lectures.

4. Merton, *No Man Is an Island*, 124.

5. Merton, *New Seeds*, 181. William Shannon's "Humility," in *The Thomas Merton Encyclopedia*, is excellent, as is Sehested, "Humility."

6. Dekar, "Power of Silence," 15–16. For a history of FOR, see my *Creating the Beloved Community: A Journey with the Fellowship of Reconciliation* (2005) and *Dangerous People: The Fellowship of Reconciliation Building a Nonviolent World of Justice, Peace, and Freedom* (2016).

5

The Power of Silence

ONE SATURDAY IN A mid-sized, mid-South city in the heartland of the United States, a few thousand people walked in silence. Lunch followed in silence.

In any conventional reading, this was not newsworthy. But it was an event. Organizers called it PeaceWalk 2002. It reverberated long after the weekend unfolded.

PeaceWalk 2002 heralded the start of a national and international uprising against the effort of allegedly powerful institutions—the US presidency, the market, and some media—to silence dissent. The rhetoric of a "war on terror" bore fruit in war against the Saddam Hussein regime in Iraq and perpetrators on September 11, 2001, of an assault that contributed to the collapse of the World Trade Towers in New York City, a partial collapse of the Pentagon, headquarters of the US Department of Defense in Arlington County, Virginia, and the downing of a fourth plane that crashed into a field in Stonycreek Township, Pennsylvania. In increasing numbers, people said "No!" to war, "not in my name!" What distinguished PeaceWalk 2002 from protests elsewhere was its demonstration of the power of silence.

On September 28, 2002, Nhat Hanh, the Vietnamese writer and peacemaker, accompanied by Sister Chân Không (Cao Ngoc Phuong) and some forty members of the Community of Mindful Living, led a mindful walk, ate a mindful lunch, and gave a mindful dharma talk, a public discourse by a respected Buddhist teacher.

PeaceWalk 2002 was well timed. War-weary, war-worried participants expressed their opposition to the war plans of those in supposedly higher places of power. In silence.

The setting—Memphis, Tennessee—was noteworthy. A century and a half earlier, the Trail of Tears began from Memphis. The US government removed the majority of Cherokee, Choctaw, and Chickasaw Indians across the Mississippi River to an imposed exile in Oklahoma Territory, which did not achieve statehood until 1907. For decades, European-Americans maintained power in Memphis through the racial intimidation and demagoguery of a political machine headed by Ed "Boss" Crump. On April 4, 1968, Martin Luther King Jr. was murdered at the Lorraine Motel, where PeaceWalk 2002 began.[1]

The most dominant features of the Memphis landscape are towering spires and imposing cathedrals of Christian congregations. Three Christian denominations are headquartered in Memphis. As well, Memphis has been the crucible by some to actualize the dream of a Christian America. Ed McAteer launched the Moral Majority in Memphis. Jerry Falwell attracted wide support in the city when he denounced Muhammad as a terrorist.

PeaceWalk 2002 represented something new to the identity of those living in and around Memphis. Crossing lines that divide—age, class, ethnicity, gender, nationality, religion, sexual orientation, and worldview—people came together. For three days, spiritual teachers led Buddhists, Christians, Hindus, Jews, Jains, Muslims, New Agers, and secular humanists who joined to walk, eat, sing, dance, listen, and meditate. They lived into Dr. King's vision of the Beloved Community, by which he spoke of the in-breaking of God's realm.

The September 27–29, 2002 weekend coincided with the opening of an expanded wing of the National Civil Rights Museum, which is housed at the Lorraine Motel. Dr. King was murdered there, and new exhibits celebrated the power of individuals, alone or collectively, to bring about change peacefully in the face of opposition by others.

On September 27th, the museum dedicated the first Eternal World Peace Flame in the United States. The torch had traveled from its permanent home at the Life Foundation International Course Center in North Wales. Hundreds lit candles from it. Dr. Mansukh Patel, author, scientist, humanitarian, and a founder of the Life Foundation Worldwide, noted the symbolism. "If we are to bring peace into this world, someone has to start, please let it be you." Chalanda Sai Ma, a spiritual leader from South India and the founder of Humanity in Unity, made a similar point. Sai Ma described PeaceWalk 2002 as a manifestation of the pilgrimage that all of us are pursuing on this planet: "We are all custodians of a tremendous energy for transformation. If we change our daily lives—the way we think, speak, and act—we begin to change the world."

---

1. For accounts, see Beifuss, *At the River I Stand*; Cobb, *Most Southern Place on Earth*; or my "I *Am* a Man."

Nhat Hanh was a keynote speaker. Introducing him, I cited words he had written in 1967:

> The people in the movement can write very good protest letters, but they are not yet able to write love letters. We need to learn to write to the Congress and to the President of the United States letters that they will not put in the trash can. We need to write the kind of letter that they will like to receive. The way you speak, the kind of language you use and the kind of understanding you express should not turn people off. Because the people you write to are also persons like all of us.

Nhat Hanh explained that mindful walking was a revolutionary way of practicing peace in the present moment. For Nhat Hanh, mindful walking or eating was essential if we want to uproot the seeds of war that germinate in our own being. To prevent war in the future, we have to practice mindfulness today. Only if we establish peace in our hearts and in our ways of looking at things, he taught, can we begin to deal with the sources of violence and war: anger, fear, hatred, misunderstanding, and possessiveness. If we wait until another war is imminent to begin to uproot these weeds from which wars take hold in our living, it will be too late.

For many participants in the Mid-South, these may have been new or fresh ideas. They chanted, "I Have Arrived" along the three and a half miles from the Lorraine Motel to Overton Park. Nhat Hanh wrote a meditation to accompany breathing with each mindful step on the route:

> I have arrived / I am home / in the here / and in the now.
>
> I have arrived / I am home / in the here / and in the now.
>
> I am solid. / I am free. / I am solid. / I am free.
>
> In the ultimate I dwell. / In the ultimate I dwell.

Nhat Hanh continued: "Take my hand. We will walk. We will only walk. We will enjoy our walk without thinking of arriving anywhere. Walk peacefully. Walk happily. Our walk is a peace walk. Our walk is a happiness walk."

Imagine the energy engendered as two thousand or more people, concentrating on these words, walked, breathed, and later ate in silence. One participant, Bob Lorsbach, commented as he arrived at the Overton Park golf course, "You think differently about speed bumps when you walk over them in mindfulness!" The long, winding, silent crowd, walking slowly, must surely have unnerved some observers along the route, and golfers.

During his dharma talk, Nhat Hanh spoke to the fear of terrorism and war. He observed that the roots of these evils—fear, hatred, misunderstanding, and violence—cannot be removed by the military. Bombs and missiles cannot reach these inner demons.

Drawing on his latest book, *Anger*, Nhat Hanh recalled that during the war in Vietnam, the people living in the United States suffered just as much as the Vietnamese people. In his poem "Call Me by My True Names," he illustrated radical empathy by recognizing himself in a frog and in the snake that eats it, then in a starving child in Uganda and in the arms merchant who sells deadly weapons there. Finally, he identified himself in a twelve-year-old girl raped by a sea pirate, and also in a sea pirate whose "heart [is] not yet capable of seeing and loving." Darkness cannot be dissipated by more darkness, he explained. Only understanding and compassion can dissolve violence and hatred.

Nhat Hanh described a current project of Plum Village in southwestern France, where he resides. The community brings together Palestinians and Israelis for retreats. The wounds of war and violence cut a wide swath and penetrate deeply. Participants do not readily identify themselves as victim and victimizer alike. Only gradually do they come to see that joy and pain are one. Only then do the doors of their hearts open.

On Sunday, September 29, Chân Không opened a Day of Mindfulness by focusing on children. She invited the youngest participants to come forward and invited everyone to reflect on the question, "How can I bring happiness to these children?" Contemplating practical questions like this, following each in-breath and each out-breath, we learned that the practice of looking deeply does not mean being inactive. We become very active when we act with love and compassion, living in such a way that a future will be possible for our children and their children.

PeaceWalk 2002 featured other distinguished speakers. Frank Thomas, pastor at the time of Mississippi Boulevard Christian Church in Memphis, was one. He quoted Martin Luther King Jr.'s April 4, 1967, address at Riverside Church in New York: "A nation that continues year after year to spend more money on military defense than on programs of social uplift is approaching spiritual death."[2]

Dr. King's declaration of eternal hostility to the giant triplets of poverty, racism, and militarism resonated with PeaceWalk 2002 participants. One concrete outcome was creation by Buddhist participants of Magnolia Grove Monastery in northwest Mississippi. Three years later, Nhat Hahn returned to participate in formally opening the 120-acre residential

2. See "Time to Break Silence" in King, *Testament of Hope*, 241.

monastery and mindfulness practice center. It has continued to serve as a place to rest with the present moment and to live peacefully with the faithful friend, our breathing.[3]

How might Thomas Merton have responded to the silence of the march? Fifty years earlier, on February 16, 1953, Thomas Merton prayed in a woodshed called St. Anne's on the trail that led a short distance from the monastery to a grove of statues. In his journal, Merton wrote of the power of silence:

> In the silence of St. Anne's everything has come together in unity and the unity is not my unity but Yours, O Father of Peace.
>
> I recognize in myself the child who walked all over Sussex. (I did not know I was looking for this shanty, or that I would one day find it.) All the countries of the world are one under this sky. I no longer need to travel. Half a mile away is the monastery with the landscape of hills which haunted me for 11 years with uncertainty. I knew I had come to stay but never really believed it, and the hills seemed to speak, at all times, of some other country.
>
> This quiet landscape of St. Anne's speaks of no other country. . . . The silence of it is making me well.[4]

Another ten years later, Merton worried, much as did PeaceWalk 2002 participants, about a looming war. In a journal entry for July 8, 1964, Merton wrote,

> There is some worry about President Johnson's policies in Asia. To make sure of votes, he has to threaten war and promise "results" against the Communists. Something very strange about a system where political power for a party demands the sacrifice of lives of poor people thousands of miles away who never heard of Democrats and Republicans! I am not talking about Communist power only, but that of Democrats or Republicans. Can I honestly vote for anyone in this year's election? The possibility of a long, stupid, costly, disastrous and pointless war in Asia is no mere phantasm. It will certainly bring no good whatever to anyone. But because it does not involve a nuclear threat to the U.S., everyone shrugs and thinks about something else.[5]

In the summer of 1964, I was active with a with community organization organizing voter registration for the upcoming federal United States

---

3. See https://magnoliagrovemonastery.org/.

4. Merton, *Search for Solitude*, 32–33.

5. Merton, *Dancing in the Water of Life*, 123–24.

election. On July 2, we celebrated passage of the Civil Rights Act, which outlawed discrimination based on race, color, religion, sex, or national origin. It prohibited unequal application of voter registration requirements, and racial segregation in schools, employment, and public accommodations. While our mood was decidedly upbeat, a wise African-American, grizzled veteran of many struggles, quietly reminded us, "We've crossed a river. There's a mountain ahead."

Nearly sixty years later, recalling PeaceWalk 2002 in the spring of 2020, I am writing at another time of tumult. The media are replete with news of worldwide pandemic, climate emergency, racial unrest, civil war in Syria, heightened military expenditure, worries about nuclear destruction, violence by some police, and genocide in Myanmar.[6]

In January 2020, the Doomsday Clock, a symbol that represents the likelihood of a human-made global catastrophe maintained since 1947 by the members of the *Bulletin of the Atomic Scientists*, was set at one hundred seconds to midnight.[7] Given our current context, one might well wonder how to respond.

On the one hand, some might experience despair, apathy, or abuse. Others might do nothing, opting, proverbially, to put their head in the sand and simply carry on. Worse, some might engage in domestic violence or self-inflict abuse by drugs, alcohol, suicide, or other dysfunctional behavior.

On the other hand, one might remember that a mountain is nothing but rock and dirt being gradually washed to the sea. Our context has engendered mutual cooperation, care, and good neighborliness. Some have dreamed and begun to identify ways to work towards a new normal, one free of poverty, a widening gap between rich and poor, and other unhealthy outcomes.

In all too many respects, our context, especially in the United States, has not changed much from when Martin Luther King Jr. anticipated that time when people might hew out of the prevailing mountain of despair a stone of hope and "transform the jangling discords of our nation into a beautiful symphony of brotherhood."[8] In early 1995, when I moved to Memphis, Tennessee, I met then Willie Herenton, who in 1991 was the first African American elected as mayor of Memphis.

Responding to Mayor Herenton's question of why I had moved to Memphis, I explained I sought to contribute to changing the image of

---

6. Wadlow, "Gambia Invokes Genocide Convention against Myanmar."

7. See https://www.defconlevel.com/doomsday-clock.php.

8. "I Have a Dream," speech delivered at the Lincoln Memorial on August 28, 1963, in King, *Testament of Hope*, 219.

Memphis. Known widely as the city where Dr. King was murdered, I saw a possible role in helping Dr. King's dream become a reality.

In his last public talk, delivered in Bangkok, Thailand on December 10, 1968 the morning before his tragic death, Merton spoke of having met some revolutionary university leaders from Europe. Merton introduced himself as a monk, to which one of the students replied, "We are monks also." Merton went on to describe the monastic vocation as taking a critical attitude toward the contemporary world and its structures. Merton saw the essential thing in monasticism as small groups attempting to love and serve God and reach union with him. Such monasticism cannot be extinguished. It is imperishable, and represents a charism given by God to us.

During PeaceWalk 2002, I grasped that vision of a full and transcendent freedom that is beyond all cultural differences and externals. The Beloved Community was breaking in. A few thousand participants claiming the power of silence hastened its unfolding. Deliberately. Mindfully.

6

Silence as Attention and Antidote

AN UNDERGRADUATE STUDENT FROM 1961 to 1965 at the University of California, Berkeley, I joined a rally on December 2, 1964. The immediate cause of the protest was a ban on distribution of leaflets on public lands. However, we students—myself included—perceived wider issues, especially the right to protest for the greater common good.

One speaker was Mario Savio, a graduate student who had spent the previous summer as a civil rights organizer in Mississippi. Savio insisted,

> There is a time when the operation of the machine becomes so odious, makes you so sick at heart that you can't take part! You can't even tacitly take part! And you've got to put your bodies upon the gears and upon the wheels, upon the levers, upon all the apparatus—and you've got to make it stop! And you've got to indicate to the people who run it, to the people who own it—that unless you're free the machine will be prevented from working at all![1]

Along with other Free Speech Movement activists, Savio claimed to be more than a cog in the corporate machinery:

> We found we were being denied the very possibility of "being a student"—unquestionably a *right*. We found we were severed from our proper roles: students denied the meaningful work one must do in order to be a student. Instead, we were faced with a situation in which the pseudo-student role we were playing was tailor-made to further the interests of those who own the University, those vast corporations in whose interest the University is managed. Time past when the skills required of laborers were

1. Savio, "Sit-in Address on the Steps of Sproul Hall"; Warshaw, *Trouble in Berkeley*, 65.

62

nowhere near so great as the ones required now, bosses built schools for their own children. Now the bosses build schools for the children of their workers . . . to further their own interests.[2]

I did not know Savio personally. In my role as a member of the student senate, I did play a small part in ending the strike. The events proved crucial for me in seeding an understanding that, to advance the common good, an activist needs to ground social action in a deep spirituality.

As mentioned in the Introduction to this book, I first read Merton when I was an undergraduate at Berkeley in the early 1960s at a time I was protesting both University of California and government policies. I resonated with Merton, who wrote an article entitled "The Root of War Is Fear" in the October 1961 issue of *The Catholic Worker*. Merton protested "true war-madness, an illness of the mind and the spirit that is spreading with a furious and subtle contagion all over the world." While conscious that the United States was not alone in its war-making madness, Merton directed his concern especially at the United States—of all the countries that are sick, the one that he saw as most "grievously afflicted."[3]

Merton insisted, "*There can be no question that unless war is abolished the world will remain constantly in a state of madness and desperation in which, because of the immense destructive power of modern weapons, the danger of catastrophe will be imminent and probably at every moment everywhere.*"[4] Merton cautioned against seeking to avoid war and to preserve peace by building bomb shelters. He saw the futility of people preparing shelters where, in case of nuclear war, they would simply bake inside slowly instead of burning up quickly by or exposure to a nuclear blast, being blown out of existence in a flash. He expressed his concern as follows: "This is a nation that claims to be fighting for religious truth along with freedom and other values of the spirit. Truly we have entered the "post-Christian era" with a vengeance. Whether we are destroyed or whether we survive, the future is awful to contemplate."[5]

Merton concluded his essay by urging Christians to be mindful that any action for peace and against war required marshalling every available resource, notably study, prayer, sacrifice, and restraint of one's instinct for violence or aggression in relations with others. "Everything else is secondary, for the survival of the human race itself depends on it. We must at least face

2. Savio, "Berkeley Student Rebellion of 1964," 86, Savio's emphasis.

3. Merton, "Root of War is Fear." I am citing the essay as published in the collection edited by Shannon: Merton, *Passion for Peace*, 11.

4. Merton, *Passion for Peace*, 12, Merton's emphasis.

5. Merton, *Passion for Peace*, 12.

this responsibility and do something about it. And the first job of all is to understand the psychological forces at work in ourselves and in society."[6]

A second article by Merton, "The Shelter Ethic," appeared the following month in *The Catholic Worker*. Merton addressed the question about the legitimacy of defending one's safety in a fallout shelter by keeping others out at the point of a gun. Merton sought to focus the discussion in the midst of what he deemed the most crucial moral and spiritual crisis the human race has ever faced during its history. Exploring the ethic of the Sermon on the Mount, Merton concluded that love and mercy, the heart of Jesus's teaching, were the most powerful forces on earth. Merton concluded,

> Let us for the love of heaven wake up to the fact that our own minds are just as filled with dangerous power today as the nuclear bombs themselves. And let us be very careful how we unleash the pent-up forces in the minds of others. The hour is extremely grave. The guarded statements of moral theologians are a small matter compared to the constant deluge of irresponsible opinions, criminal half-truths and murderous images disseminated by the mass media. The struggle for survival, freedom and truth is going to be won or lost in our thoughts, in our spirit. It is because the minds of men have become what they have become that the world is poised on the brink of total disaster.[7]

In the 1950s, his second decade as a monk, Merton grew increasingly concerned to overcome the busy-ness and noisy-ness that threatened to inundate life at Gethsemani. As antidote, Merton nurtured spiritual practices of silence and solitude. At the time he entered the monastery at Gethsemani, silence very much dominated the way of life. Monks communicated by signs and rarely spoke apart from the daily office and liturgies. As did all the monks, Merton prayed in silence and withdrew in silence to walk and meditate in nature.

In a book entitled *The Monastic Journey*, Merton wrote of the "basic principles of monastic spirituality." Merton reflected on a "need of monastic silence, that the monk may be 'swift to hear and slow to speak' (James 1:19)."[8] He characterized the monastic vocation as a calling to a life of penance, renunciation, stillness, solitude, and silence. Merton wrote of solitude as "so necessary both for society and for the individual that when society fails to provide sufficient solitude to develop the inner life of the persons who compose it,

6. Merton, *Passion for Peace*, 13.

7. Merton, *Passion for Peace*, 26.

8. Merton, *Monastic Journey*, 50. William H. Shannon wrote excellent articles on silence and solitude for *The Thomas Merton Encyclopedia*, 433–35 and 443–44.

they rebel and seek false solitudes . . . which locks the door against all men and pores over its own private accumulation of rubbish."[9] Continuing, Merton deemed silence a prerequisite to spiritual growth.

> If we fill our lives with silence, then we live in hope, and Christ lives in us and gives our virtues much substance. Then, when the time comes, we confess Him openly before men, and our confession has much meaning because it is rooted in deep silence. It awakens the silence of Christ in the hearts of those who hear us, so that they themselves fall silent and begin to wonder and to listen. For they have begun to discover their true selves.[10]

In an essay entitled "Rain and the Rhinoceros," Merton wrote of

> . . . a whole world of meaning . . . of silence . . . Think of it: all that speech pouring down, selling nothing, judging nobody . . . washing out the places where men have stripped the hillside! What a thing it is to sit absolutely alone, in the forest, at night, cherished by this wonderful, unintelligible, perfectly innocent speech, the most comforting speech in the world, the talk that rain makes by itself all over the ridges, and the talk of the watercourses everywhere in the hollows![11]

In an essay entitled "Apologies to an Unbeliever," Merton characterized his particular task in the church and in the world as that of

> the solitary explorer who, instead of jumping on all the latest bandwagons at once, is bound to search the existential depths of faith in its silences, its ambiguities, and in those certainties which lie deeper than the bottom of anxiety . . . a kind of submarine life in which faith sometimes mysteriously takes on the aspect of doubt when, in fact, one has to doubt and reject conventional and superstitious surrogates that have taken the place of faith.[12]

Merton rarely described his own experience of silence. He did respond to Abdul Aziz, a Pakistani Sufi (a stream of Islam that nurtures direct personal experience of the Holy), who first wrote Merton in 1960. A lively correspondence developed between the two men. On January 2, 1966, Merton explained that he had a very simple way of prayer centered entirely on attention to the presence of God, God's will, and God's love.

---

9. Merton, *No Man Is an Island*, 247–48.

10. Merton, *No Man Is an Island*, 259. This passage is in a chapter on silence, 254–64.

11. Merton, *Raids on the Unspeakable*, 10.

12. Merton, *Faith and Violence*, 213.

Drawing comparisons with practices of Muslims, Merton wrote that his prayers grew from faith and silence:

> My meditation [has] the character described by the Prophet as "being before God as if you saw Him." Yet it does not mean imagining anything or conceiving a precise image of God, for to my mind this would be a kind of idolatry. On the contrary, it is a matter of adoring Him as invisible and infinitely beyond our comprehension, and realizing Him as all. My prayer tends very much toward what you call *fana*. There is in my heart this great thirst to recognize totally the nothingness of all that is not God. My prayer is then a kind of praise rising up out of the center of Nothing and Silence. If I am still present "myself" this I recognize as an obstacle about which I can do nothing unless He Himself removes the obstacle. If He wills He can then make the Nothingness into a total clarity. If He does not will, then the Nothingness seems to itself to be an object and remains an obstacle. Such is my ordinary way of prayer, or meditation. It is not "thinking about" anything, but a direct seeking of the Face of the Invisible, which cannot be found unless we become lost in Him who is Invisible[13]

Merton chafed at business aspects of monastic life and activity that undermined his desire to spend more time in silence, stillness, and solitude. Recognizing this need, Abbot James Fox granted Merton use of an abandoned shed, which Merton called "St. Anne's" and to which he could withdraw for prayer, meditation, or contemplation. Merton noted,

> It is a tremendous thing no longer to have to debate in my mind about "being a hermit," even though I am not one. At least now solitude is something concrete—it is "St. Anne's"—the long view of hills, the empty cornfields in the bottoms, the crows in the trees, and the cedars bunched together on the hillside. And when I am here there is always lots of sky and lots of peace and I don't have distractions and everything is serene . . . Here there seems to be less and less need even of books.[14]

Merton affirmed the importance of silence: "I need very much this silence and this snow. Here alone can I find my way because here alone the way is right in front of my face, and it is God's way for me—there is really no

---

13. Merton, *Essential Writings*, 82, Merton's emphasis.
14. Merton, *Search for Solitude*, 29, entry for February 9, 1953.

other."[15] In *Thoughts in Solitude*, Merton included the prayer that is perhaps most often quoted:

> My Lord God, I have no idea where I am going. I do not see the road ahead of me. I cannot know for certain where it will end. Nor do I really know myself, and the fact that I think that I am following your will does not mean that I am actually doing so. But I believe that the desire to please you does in fact please you. And I hope I have that desire in all that I am doing. I hope that I will never do anything apart from that desire. And I know that if I do this you will lead me by the right road, though I may know nothing about it. Therefore will I trust you always though I may seem to be lost and in the shadow of death. I will not fear, for you are ever with me, and you will never leave me to face my perils alone.[16]

Merton has continued to give spiritual direction to me and others who discern computers, mobile phones, and other technological gizmos as an "addiction." The success of Kathleen Norris's *The Cloister Walk* (1996) and Philip Groaning's *Into Great Silence* (German: *Die große Stille*) attest to a deep malaise and need in Western society. The latter is a documentary film that provides an intimate portrait of the everyday lives of Carthusian monks at *Grande Chartreuse,* a monastery high in the French Alps (Chartreuse Mountains).

Locally, along with many fellow activists, I have felt deeply the need to act on a biblical priority, "Be still, and know that I am God: I am exalted among the nations; I am exalted in the earth" [Psalm 46:10]. In the mid-1980s a number of us agreed to meet once a week at seven in the morning for an hour of prayer. We could not discuss social issues, nor plan anything. We devoted an hour to silence, solitude, and stillness. Often God spoke to one of us in powerful ways, which we shared with one another. Once a month, one of us, in one of our homes, would host a breakfast during which our families joined us. During activities organized by the Hamilton Disarmament Coalition, of which I was cochair, we marched under a "Peace Prayer Group" banner and invited others to join us in setting aside time for reflection, renewal, and recreation.[17]

---

15. Merton, *Turning towards the World*, 295, entry for January 28, 1963.

16. Merton, *Thoughts in Solitude*, 79. Kate Campbell with Spooner Oldham records the prayer on *For the Living of These Days* (2006).

17. A Mennonite participant, Hugo Neufeld, has written a brief account in *The North End Lives*, 124.

More recently, I have been involved in Culture of Peace Hamilton, an offshoot of the United Nations Association in Canada. We have worked for nearly two decades to apply six pathways locally. These call for respecting life; helping, not hurting; taking care of children; protecting the environment; sharing resources; listening to others with respect; and reducing violence, especially towards women and the vulnerable.[18]

These commitments resonate with Merton, whose writings on prayer, contemplation, and meditation have nourished me. Merton called people to "true prayer . . . every moment is a new discovery of a new silence, a new penetration into that eternity in which all things are always new. We know, by fresh discovery, the deep reality that is our concrete existence here and now and in the depths of that reality we receive from the Father light, truth, wisdom and peace. These are the reflection of God in our souls which are made to His image and likeness."[19]

18. See https://cultureofpeacehamilton.com/.

19. Merton, *Thoughts in Solitude*, 97–98.

7

Divinization in Merton

DIVINIZATION OR DEIFICATION MEANS union, participation, communion, partnership, adoption, re-creation, similitude, rebirth, regeneration, or transfiguration into divine image and likeness. The word expresses a central Christian teaching that at creation, God so cared for humankind that God endowed us with the divine nature. Genesis 1:26–28 introduces the idea of *imago Dei* (image of God), as follows:

> Then God said, "Let us make humankind in our image, according to our likeness; and let them have dominion over the fish of the sea, and over the birds of the air, and over the cattle, and over all the wild animals of the earth, and over every creeping thing that creeps upon the earth." So God created humankind in his image, in the image of God he created them; male and female he created them. God blessed them, and said to them, "'Be fruitful and multiply . . .'"

Christians believe that in Christ, God lived a fully human life. Following Jesus, who cited Psalm 82:6, we are to take on God's character: "Is it not written in your law, 'I said, you are gods'?" (John 10:34). In the Sermon on the Mount, Jesus called on his followers to imitate God: "I say to you, Love your enemies and pray for those who persecute you, so that you may be children of your Father in heaven . . . Be perfect, therefore, as your Father in heaven is perfect" (Matt 5:44–45, 48). God dwells within: "For all who are led by the Spirit of God are children of God" (Rom 8:14). We are like Jesus: "See what love the Father has given us that we should be called children of God; and that is what we are" (1 John 3:1).

The biblical *locus classicus* of deification is 2 Peter 1:3–8. The text affirms our participation in the divine nature:

> [God's] divine power has given us everything needed for life and godliness, through the knowledge of him who called us by his own glory and goodness. Thus he has given us, through these things, his precious and very great promises, so that through them you may escape from the corruption that is in the world because of lust, and may become participants in the divine nature. For this very reason, you must make every effort to support your faith with goodness, and goodness with knowledge, and knowledge with self-control, and self-control with endurance, and endurance with godliness, and godliness with mutual affection, and mutual affection with love. For if these things are yours and are increasing among you, they keep you from being ineffective and unfruitful in the knowledge of our Lord Jesus Christ.

Among noncanonical texts, the writer of *The Gospel of Thomas* asserts that followers of Jesus, wishing to return to the heavenly realm whence they have come, appear not to be fully human. They have come from the light, "the place where the light has come into being by itself, has established [itself] and has appeared in their image . . . the sign of your Father among you . . . is movement and repose."[1]

In the second century of the Common Era, Bishop Irenaeus of Lyons taught that the process of salvation from creation to the end of time is a work of grace from one God. Humans share fully in the divine nature and likeness. "The glory of God is man fully alive, and the life of man is the vision of God. If the revelation of God through creation already brings life to all living beings on the earth, how much more will the manifestation of the Father by the Word bring life to those who see God."[2]

Other Christian writers explored the deification theme. Athanasius of Alexandria (ca. 296–373) observed God became human to make Adam a God. A century later, in 451, church leaders convened an ecumenical council at Chalcedon, a city on the Asian side of the Bosporus—Istanbul today—and upheld a growing consensus that Jesus, truly God and truly human, is unique, precious, and holy, the fullness of the divine image

---

1. Thomas 50, in Patterson, Robinson, and Bethge, *Fifth Gospel*, 12. The text inspired *Man Alive*, a documentary and current affairs series that ran on BBC2 between 1965 and 1981, and a column by a *Toronto Star* journalist, Tom Harpur (1930–2017), whose book *The Pagan Christ* (2004) renewed early Christian controversies about Jesus.

2. Irenaeus, *Against Heresies*, 4.20.7 and 4.35.5–7 (*ANF*, 490, 507). Another translation emphasizes that we, like the Son, are made in God's image and likeness. See Richardson, *Early Christian Fathers*, 397. For an example of papal use of this teaching, see Delhaye, "Pope John Paul II on the Contemporary Importance of St. Irenaeus." For a historical survey, see Ackroyd and Evans, *The Cambridge History of the Bible: From the Beginnings to Jerome.*

and likeness. In creed, they confessed, "Christ, Son, Lord, Only-begotten, recognized in two natures, without confusion, without change, without division, without separation . . . is the one and the same Son and Only-begotten God the Word, Lord Jesus Christ."[3]

A concrete manifestation of this idea that Jesus and all humans bear two natures is incorporated in Christian icons.[4] Meditating on an icon, a devotee is open to experiencing transformation and may be led to see him or herself not through the perspective of sin, but as one whose divine image and likeness have been restored through Christ. Since 1054, when the schism between the Eastern and Western Christian churches deepened, Orthodox Christians tended to use icons in worship to a greater extent than Latin Christians.

In the sixteenth century, insisting on *sola scriptura* (Latin for "by scripture alone"), major Protestant pastors including Martin Luther and John Calvin affirmed the idea of *imago Dei* that humans bear true godliness. Both attacked icons.[5] A century later the English poet George Herbert (1593–1633) summarized in one line, "In Christ two natures met to be thy cure."[6]

Thomas Merton immersed himself in such biblical and theological language. Especially from 1951 to 1955, when he served as master of scholastics, then as novice master until 1965 Merton studied the theology of eastern Christians and the ideas of *theōsis* or divinization. He developed the deification idea principally in *The New Man*, a "crucial text for grasping Merton's essentially Christian theological vision."[7] Although Merton developed the theme throughout his considerable output, *The New Man* presented his most sustained exploration of Christology. In a chapter entitled "the war within us," Merton wrote, "Life and death are at war within us. . . . All truly religious thought claims to arm man for his struggle with death with weapons that will ensure the victory of life over death."[8]

In language that resonates with key ideas of Irenaeus, Athanasius, and other early Christian writers, Merton asserts that in Christ, humankind has conquered death and enjoys eternal life as divinized being. One is in effect a totally new creation, having come to orient his or her being and to "subsist

---

3. Pelikan, *Emergence of the Catholic Tradition (100-600)*, 263–66; Bettenson, *Documents of the Christian Church*, 51–52; McGrath, *Historical Theology*, 55–61.

4. Payton, *Light from the Christian East*, ch. 11; Ware, *Orthodox Church*, 38.

5. Luther, *Catholic Epistles*, 153–54; Calvin, *Inst.* 3.11.10.

6. See "Offering," stanza 1, in Herbert, *Country Parson; The Temple*, 271.

7. Cunningham, *Thomas Merton and the Monastic Vision*, 81; Shannon, "New Man," 322–23. Merton's unpublished notes on "Oikonomia and Deification" are available at the Thomas Merton Center, Bellarmine University, Louisville, Kentucky.

8. Merton, *New Man*, 1–2.

outside the individual self in the Absolute—in Christ, in God."[9] To find fulfillment and discover one's true self, one must become wholly and entirely
alive, allowing oneself to experience the peaceful integration of all one's powers into one perfect actuality that is one's true self.

> It is this perfect self-realization by contact of our own anguished
> freedom with the life-giving Freedom of Him Who is Holy and
> Unknown that man begins the conquest of death in his own soul.
> This finding of our true self, this awakening, this coming to life in
> the luminous darkness of the infinite God, can never be anything
> but a communion with God by the grace of Jesus Christ. Our
> victory over death is not our own work, but His. The triumph of
> our own freedom, which must truly be *our* triumph if it is to save
> us from death, is nevertheless also and primarily His.[10]

Crucially, humans need not wait until the afterlife to enjoy the fruits
of life in Christ. In our earthly flesh, we are united with God. Merton calls
this deification, the ultimate in human self-realization and transformation.
Discovering our true self, we find ourselves mystically one with the God by
Whom we are elevated and transformed.

> The union of the Christian with God is . . . nothing else but a
> participation in the life, and wisdom, and joy of peace of God
> Himself. This is greater than any other gift, higher than any
> other power. It is supreme freedom, the most perfect fulfillment.
> It has been called by the Fathers of the Church the *divinization
> (theosis)* of man. It is the ultimate in man's self-realization, for
> when it is perfected, man not only discovers his true self, but
> finds himself to be mystically one with the God by Whom he has
> been elevated and transformed.[11]

In a chapter entitled "Image and Likeness," Merton explores a theme
that dominates his writing over the last ten years of his life. Our truest self-
hood resembles God insofar as our creativity, inseparable from our nature,
is the image and likeness—in which the image is perfected in a completely
faithful correspondence to its original. We create a society that is an extension
of the sanctified spirit of humans, in which all creation praises God.

Upholding an understanding that the "image of God is found in
the person's very structure—awareness, thought, love," Merton makes the
staggering claim that "we are ourselves Christ. In us, the image of God is

9. Merton, *New Man*, 6.

10. Merton, *New Man*, 8–9, Merton's emphasis.

11. Merton, *New Man*, 27, Merton's emphasis.

complete and entire in each individual . . . . We are [God's] new Paradise. And in the midst of that Paradise stands Christ Himself, the Tree of life. From the base of the tree the four rivers of Eden flow out to irrigate . . . the whole word. . . . We are in the world as Christ-bearers and temples of the Holy Spirit, because our souls are filled with his grace."[12]

Merton touches on the deification theme in other writings. In *New Seeds of Contemplation*, he writes, "To say that I am made in the image of God is to say that love is the reason for my existence, for God is love. Love is my true identity. Selflessness is my true self. Love is my true character. Love is my name."[13] In *The Ascent to Truth*, a study of contemplative prayer according in the writings of the Spanish mystic John of the Cross, Merton affirms,

> Christ was not a wise man who came to teach a doctrine. He is God, Who became incarnate in order to effect a mystical trans-formation of mankind . . . . The teaching of Christ is the seed of a new life. Reception of the word of God by faith initiates man's transformation. It elevates him above this world and above his own nature and transports his acts of thought and of desire to a supernatural level. He becomes a partaker of the divine nature, a Son of God, and Christ is living in him.[14]

Peter Brown, a scholar of late antiquity (from 150 to 750), tells the story of one of the most illustrious of the desert saints. Someone asked Symeon Stylites, "Are you human?" The holy man answered that he was deliberately not so! Standing apart from ties of kinship or of economics, he was "a stranger among men without being possessed by a god."[15]

This story segues with Merton's insights on divinization. This pro-foundly countercultural insight can be a source of resilience in the face of the tsunami of noise and materialism that has swept over the developed west and north, and that now fuels a surge of consumerism in newly devel-oping countries such as Brazil, China, and India.

Thomas Merton is known best in relation to Christian dialogue with adherents of other religions, especially those of Asia, liturgical reform, and renewed interest in prayer and other spiritual practices. Merton is not generally included among the great Christian theologians.[16] Under-valued

---

12. Merton, *New Man*, 94–95.

13. Merton, *New Seeds of Contemplation*, 60.

14. Merton, *Ascent of Truth*, 11; Merton, *Thomas Merton Reader*, 378.

15. Brown, "Holy Man in Late Antiquity," 93.

16. The late Yale scholar Jaroslav Pelikan did not cite Merton in his magisterial, five-volume history of Christian doctrine. In a history of the Catholic Church, another magisterial, five-volume study, Roger Aubert mentions Merton in a footnote in relation

outside the monastery as the brilliant theologian he was, Merton's theological acumen led him to his teaching role at the Abbey of Gethsemani as master of scholastics from 1951 to 1955 and as novice master until 1965. Merton had an uncanny ability to synthesize the great tradition in Western thought from the earliest Christian centuries through the renewal movements of the twentieth century and to explain complex ideas in an accessible manner. Merton also engaged significantly with contemporary theological trends including emergent theologies of liberation in Latin America, a theme discussed more fully in chapter 10.

Merton's writings also have pastoral significance, especially regarding our true self. I offer a story from a friend's therapy practice as evidence. (The source is protected.)

> I had "a mum" and "a young nineteen-year-old sibling" on my couch here last eve—both bereaved after the sudden traumatic death of their twenty-three-year-old daughter and sister—just eight weeks ago.
>
> This young man's mother bought him to see me as she was anxious about his upcoming travel overseas. She shared fears that he may come to harm while away—maybe even die in some sort of accident (no surprise here).
>
> The young man said to me as we were coming to the close of our time together, "So, tell me about Thomas Merton." I smiled and said "Oh, you see the books opposite you on my desk." He said, "Well, I counted around eleven in that pile!" We laughed together.
>
> I briefly shared a little about Merton and my interest in the Trappists' way of life. His mum said—"there you go son—off to look up Merton!"
>
> Traumatic death . . . them on my couch and Merton books on my sideboard.

A twofold grip holds many hostages in contemporary society. The first is a technology that has come to be for many a necessity. In North America and throughout the world, many people go about their daily routines with cellphone in hand. They are often oblivious to everything else about them.

The second has to do with finances. Despite warnings sounded by government officials that people have too great a personal debt load, people continue to spend beyond their limit.

Merton offers an alternative path for the human community. To flourish and cohere within the common weal, Merton urges us to be concerned

---

to the increase of vocations to the Trappist order. Aubert, *Church in a Secularised Society*, 282n41

about the "common good," the well-being of the entire "family of man," title of a photography exhibition first shown in 1955 at the Museum of Modern Art in New York City. In a society that seems to value the material to the loss of the spiritual, and the individual to the loss of community, Merton provides a compass for the rudderless, the alienated, and the hesitant, whose ships need direction. These may be good ships, but are otherwise lost. Early in his Christian journey, Merton thought he could never be a saint.[17] While I am unaware of an effort to promote his canonization, Merton has rightly become a spiritual guide for twenty-first-century people.

Merton immersed himself in writings that brought him into dialogue with the teachings of the Christian churches of the East, and of Eastern religion. Merton understood that grace works in and through us, thus carrying out so real and radical a change of heart and life that the divine image is in us. Clothed with the light of divine likeness, we are able to recognize the same in others and thus to love and live in simplicity and unity.[18]

For Merton, "because God became man, because every man is potentially Christ, because Christ is our brother, and because we have no right to let our brother live in want, or in any form of squalor whether physical or spiritual." Merton insisted that "if we really understood the meaning of Christianity in social life, we would see it as part of the redemptive work of Christ, liberating man from misery, squalor, subhuman living conditions, economic or political slavery, ignorance, alienation."[19] By grace, God enables every person to actualize her or his deepest self. Discovering this true self, one becomes the new creation God intended each of us to be.

17. Merton, *Seven Storey Mountain*, 237–38. See Bochen, "Sanctity," 399–401.

18. Merton, *Introduction to Christian Mysticism*, 126, 128.

19. Merton, *Conjectures of a Guilty Bystander*, 81–82.

Section Four: **Merton's Embrace of "the Other"**

Introduction

ACADEMICS HAVE GIVEN ATTENTION to how we craft "the Other." In *Encountering "the Other"* the late Ecumenical Patriarch Athenogoras of Constantinople (1886–1972) wrote,

> I just want to welcome and to share. I don't hold onto my ideas and projects. If someone shows me something better—no, I shouldn't say better, but good—I accept them without any regrets. I no longer seek to compare. What is good, true and real is always for me the best.[1]

Developing this theme, I have benefitted from writings by Edward Said (1935–2003), Palestinian-born professor of literature at Colombia University; Edith Wyshogrod (1930–2009), who taught primarily at Rice University and published on ethical themes such as justice in light of technologically assisted mass death; and Miraslav Volf (b. 1956), Croatian-born theologian who cites the loving father's embrace of his prodigal son as illustrative of God's forgiving love and embrace of an errant humanity.

In *Us and Them: A History of Intolerance in America*, Jim Carnes provides case studies of the history and psychology of intolerance in the United States. Carnes concludes,

> Though as a nation we have often failed to acknowledge it, our strength has always arisen from our diversity. America's great achievements—in art, in literature, in science and government—have come about because we were open to new peoples, new ideas, new visions. Throughout our history, individuals and groups have made great sacrifices for the cause of freedom

---

1. Cited in Vanier, *Encountering "the Other,"* 5.

and equality. Their example can inspire us to learn to live together in harmony.[2]

In the thirty years since Carnes wrote the book, much has changed,
yet racial strife persists. Thomas Merton—a white man living in the South—
would not have been surprised. Though he rarely met people of different
nationalities or ethnicities, he expressed great concern about diversity in his
journals, correspondence, and publications during the 1950s and 1960s. At
a deep level, he embraced "the Other" as essential to his identity.

> If I can unite *in myself* the thought and the devotion of Eastern
> and Western Christendom, the Greek and the Latin Fathers,
> the Russians with the Spanish mystics, I can prepare in myself
> the reunion of divided Christians. From that secret and unspo-
> ken unity in myself can eventually come a visible and manifest
> unity of all Christians. If we want to bring together what is
> divided, we can not do so by imposing the one division upon
> the other or absorbing one division into the other or absorbing
> one division into the other. But if we do this, the union is not
> Christian. We must contain all divided worlds in ourselves and
> transcend them in Christ.[3]

Thomas Merton was ahead of his time in analyzing structures that
sustained racism and disunity. He acknowledged his duty and the responsibility of all Christians to discern truth in what people of color called for
in liberation struggles. This section includes three articles that highlight
Merton's embrace of "the Other." Chapter 8 imagines a brief dialogue that
might have ensued had the retreat occurred as planned to bring together
three "blessed peacemakers."[4] "Thich Nhat Hanh, Martin Luther King, Jr.
and Thomas Merton on Retreat" first appeared in *Weavings* (2014). When
I read it at an ITMS gathering, I invited two Shannon Fellows to assist. Dr.
King's account of violence led the student who read his words to weep.
Assuring her this was an apt response to manifest evil, I consoled her. We
waited until she could continue.

2. Carnes, *Us and Them*, 127.

3. Merton, *Conjectures of a Guilty Bystander,* 21, Merton's emphasis.

4. Walters and Jarrell, *Blessed Peacemakers: 365 Extraordinary People Who Changed
the World*, includes entries for Nhat Hahn (October 11), Dr. King (April 4), and Merton
(December 10), as well as others discussed in this book, including Daniel and Philip
Berrigan (May 17 and October 5), Dorothy Day (November 8), Catherine Doherty
(August 17), Gandhi (October 2), A. J. Muste (February 20), and Micah (October 25),
citing the text shaping this book.

I wrote the second essay in this section, "Merton on Gandhi," for a book to be published in late 2021, *Merton and Hinduism*, edited by David Odorisio. The conference for which final essay in this section, "Thomas Merton's Embrace of 'the Other' in Letters with Ernesto Cardenal," was to be read in June 2021 at St. Mary's College in Notre Dame, Indiana, and has been re-scheduled.

8

Thich Nhat Hanh, Martin Luther King Jr., and Thomas Merton on Retreat

AFTER A SPEAKING ENGAGEMENT in Memphis, Tennessee, Martin Luther King Jr. planned to continue to the Abbey of Our Lady of Gethsemani in Kentucky, where he would join Thich Nhat Hanh and Thomas Merton on retreat. On April 4, 1968, having visited the Pleasant Hill Shaker community in eastern Kentucky, Merton learned of Dr. King's murder. Stopping by the roadside, Merton thought, "I could cry." The next day, at his hermitage, Merton said a Mass for Dr. King and wrote Coretta Scott King to express grief, shock, and prayerful concern.[1]

The following "transcript" imagines the dialogue that might have ensued had the three men met together. Ordained in their respective traditions as teacher, pastor, or priest, each prayed and participated in other practices for his own spiritual fulfillment. Each undertook retreats for refreshment and spiritual growth. Each sought to help others to live compassionately.

Welcoming his guests, Merton began as follows:

TM: People are suffering for want of compassion, a quality at the heart in our respective traditions. Compassion calls us to honor our common humanity. In language of the Religious Society of Friends, or Quakers, the spiritual community of my mother Ruth Jenkins Merton, this means respecting that of God in every person. Within everyone is a spark of the Divine. Friends speak of an Inner Light and seek guidance and comfort from this Light through silent worship and active service.[2]

---

1. Merton, *Other Side of the Mountain*, 79, entry for April 5, 1968; Apel, "Crisis, of Faith."

2. "Do you behave with brotherly love to all men whatever their race, background or opinion? Do you try to make the stranger feel at home among you?" *Advices and Queries*, #22.

TNH: We need to cultivate compassion as an antidote to contemporary processes that foster suffering such as consumerism, militarism, environmental decline, individualism, and the collapse of community.

MLK: Compassion is at the heart of the campaigns in which I have played a role. In 1954, I assumed the pastorate of Dexter Avenue Baptist Church in Montgomery, Alabama. On December 1, 1955, a seamstress named Rosa Parks was arrested for violating segregation laws. Her action precipitated civil disobedience that lasted over a year. The movement had qualities of the monastic life. We maintained spiritual disciplines such as inner silence, simplicity, speaking truth to power, and disarming our hearts. We resolved to experience evil through suffering, not by exacerbating or creating negative forces.

As the bus boycott dragged on, I received threats. One night toward the end of January, 1956, I was about to doze off when the telephone rang. An angry voice said, "Listen nigger, we've taken all we want from you; before next week you'll be sorry you ever came to Montgomery."

Restless, I bowed my head over my kitchen table and prayed aloud. The words I spoke to God that midnight are still vivid in my memory: Lord, I'm down here trying to do what's right. I think I'm right. I am here taking a stand for what I believe is right. But Lord, I must confess that I'm weak now, I'm faltering. I've come to the point where I can't face it alone. Then it seemed though I could hear the quiet assurance of God saying, "Martin Luther, stand up for righteousness. Stand up for justice. Stand up for truth. And lo, I will be with you. Even until the end of the world." All uncertainty dissipated. I was ready to face anything.[3]

TM: A few years ago, a peace activist wrote me, asking for some thoughts that might guide his involvement for peace. I cautioned against depending on the hope for results, but in the value, the rightness, the truth of the work. I encouraged him to free himself from cultural norms and not to value profit or success, but rather simply to serve Christ's truth.

Our real hope, then, is not in something we think *we* can do but in *God* who is making something good out of it in some way we cannot see. If we can do God's will, we will be helping in this process. But we will not necessarily know all about it before hand.[4]

TNH: I hope we can bring a new dimension to the peace movement, which is filled with people who are angry, who hate. Neither can fulfill the path we expect from them. A fresh way of being peace, of doing peace is

3. King, *Autobiography*, 77–78.

4. See "Letter to a Peacemaker [Jim Forest]" in Merton, *Essential Writings*, 135–36, Merton's emphasis.

needed. That is why it is so important for us to practice meditation, to acquire the capacity to look, to see, and to understand. By our meeting together, we can contribute to the peace movement a unique way of looking at things. This can diminish aggression and hatred. Peace work means being peace. Meditation is for all of us. We rely on each other. Our children are relying on us that they may have a brighter future.[5]

MLK: We are made for that which is high and noble and good. I cannot hate my enemies. How can we make compassion a positive force in the world? Five years ago, as a number of us tried to cross the Edmund Pettus Bridge on the Selma-Montgomery road, Sheriff Jim Clark met us with horses, billy clubs, dogs and tear gas. March 7, 1965, armed police attacked and brutally beat civil rights movement demonstrators as we attempted to march to Montgomery. One of the marchers called out, "Do you love Martin King?" "Certainly Lord," responded the people. "Do you love Martin King?" "Certainly Lord." And again, "Do you love Martin King?" "Certainly, certainly, certainly, Lord."

The young minister then called out, "Do you love [Sheriff] Jim Clark?" Silence. "Do you love Jim Clark?" A few responded with a muffled "Certainly Lord." The civil rights leader asked a third time, "Do you love Jim Clark?" As the point sank in, the crowd responded "Certainly, certainly, certainly, Lord."

As Jesus commanded us to love our enemies, in this situation, we understood that it was insufficient to defeat Jim Clark. We wanted Clark to convert. We cannot win by hating. To effect change, we must love.[6]

TM: We are all participants in the Divine Nature, from which flows goodness, knowledge, self-control, endurance, godliness, mutual affection, and love. This very great gift has enabled me to become one in union with the God of love and to reach out to others (2 Pet 1:3-7).

TNH: The monastic life has helped me to work for changes in society, to make it more livable. For those who are alienated or uprooted, the monastic life is not an escape but rather one viable path by which to become a beacon of hope, light, and love for others.

MLK: War is a poor chisel from which to carve out peaceful tomorrows. As religious leaders in our respective traditions, we have an obligation to awaken on the part of our fellow Christians and Buddhists a spirituality of engagement rooted in each tradition. During the Birmingham campaign, participants signed the following pledge:

5. Nhat Hahn, *Being Peace*, 80.

6. Wink, *Powers That Be*, 176–77, and King, *Autobiography*, 270–89, for the Selma campaign.

I hereby pledge myself—my person and my body—to the nonviolent movement. Therefore I will keep the following ten commandments:

1. Meditate daily on the teachings and life of Jesus.

2. Remember always that the nonviolent movement in Birmingham seeks justice and reconciliation—not victory.

3. Walk and talk in the manner of love, for God is love.

4. Pray daily to be used by God in order that all men [and women] might be free.

5. Sacrifice personal wishes in order that all men [and women] might be free.

6. Observe with both friend and foe the ordinary rules of courtesy.

7. Seek to perform regular service for others and for the world.

8. Refrain from the violence of fist, tongue, or heart.

9. Strive to be in good spiritual and bodily health.

10. Follow the directions of the movement and of the captain of a demonstration.

Print Name _____

Signature _____ [7]

TNH: Let us recall a parable of the Russian writer Leo Tolstoy. A king wanted answers to what he regarded as the three most important questions in life. When is the best time to do each thing? Who are the most important people to work with? What is the most important thing to do at all times? Several people replied, but the emperor was unsatisfied. He went to a hermit known to be enlightened. *En route,* someone attacked the emperor before falling with a deep gash. Disregarding why he had sought out the hermit, the emperor cleaned his assailant's wound.

Later, the emperor turned to the hermit for an answer to his three questions. The hermit replied that they had already been answered. The most important time was the here and now. The most important person and pursuit were to care for the injured party. If all our friends in service

---

7. Pledge of nonviolence written by King and signed by those who marched in Birmingham and Selma, 1963. See "Why We Can't Wait" in King, *Testament of Hope,* 537.

communities of any kind do not love and help one another, who can we love and care for?[8]

TM: We are brothers. Our presence together today is a sign of our interdependence.

[A bell rings.]

TM: The ringing of the monastery's bell is a reminder that it is time for Compline. It has been a good day. But before we pause for communal prayer and sleep, I would like to pray:

> Almighty and merciful God, Father of all, Creator and Ruler of the Universe, Lord of History, whose designs are inscrutable, whose glory is without blemish, whose compassion for our errors is inexhaustible, in your will is our peace.
>
> Mercifully look upon us, hear our prayer which rises to you from the tumult and desperation of a world in which you are forgotten, in which your name is not invoked, your laws are derided, and your presence is ignored.
>
> From the heart of an eternal silence, you are present to us, on retreat, and when we go our separate ways, may our time together serve to encourage others to travel a road that leads to justice, liberty, and a deep sense of friendship and mutuality.
>
> Above all, grant us understanding that our ways are not necessarily your ways; that we cannot fully penetrate the mystery of your designs; and that the very storm of power now raging on this earth reveals your hidden will and your inscrutable decisions. Lighten our journey through this this cosmic storm. May we seek peace where it is truly to be found, in your will and your ways. All praise be to you, O God, our peace! Amen.[9]

Personal Reflections

Thomas Merton, Martin Luther King Jr., and Nhat Hanh have long influenced my faith and shaped my efforts to work for a better world. Committed to nonviolent social change, I joined the Fellowship of Reconciliation (FOR) in the mid-1960s. All three men had an association with FOR. I received two postcards of welcome. Words of Dr. King were on one: "A nation that continues year after year to spend more money on military defense than on programs of social uplift is approaching spiritual death."[10]

8. Nhat Hahn, *Miracle of Being Awake*, 17.

9. Adapted from Merton's prayer read in the US House of Representatives, April 12, 1962. Merton, *Essential Writings*, 137–39.

10. See "Time to Break Silence" in King, *Testament of Hope*, 241. See my *Creating*

Dr. King spoke these words at Riverside Church on April 4, 1967. He urged students—as I was at the time—to give up an automatic draft deferment. I was led to go before my draft board as a conscientious objector and subsequently to serve a period of alternative service in West Africa.

Words of Nhat Hanh graced the second card:

> The people in the movement can write very good protest letters, but they are not yet able to write love letters. We need to learn to write to the Congress and to the President of the United States letters that they will not put in the trash can. We need to write the kind of letter that they will like to receive. The way you speak, the kind of language you use and the kind of understanding you express should not turn people off. Because the people you write to are also persons like all of us.

Years later, I attended the opening of the Martin Luther King Jr. Center for Nonviolent Social Change in Atlanta, Georgia, where I signed a "Living the Dream" pledge. I carry a copy in my wallet. It reads, "I pledge to do everything that I can to make America and the world a place where equality and justice, freedom and peace will grow and flourish. On January 20, 1986, I commit myself to living the dream by loving, not hating, showing understanding, not anger, making peace, not war."

On September 28, 2002, in Memphis, Tennessee, several thousand persons gathered at the Lorraine Motel where Martin Luther King Jr. was murdered. Nhat Hanh lit a flame and, with Cao Ngoc Phuong and other spiritual leaders, led a walk some ten miles to a mid-city park. What distinguished the walk? Everyone walked in silence. At the park, people ate, again in silence. Only later, in a public talk, did Nhat Hanh break the silence.

Organized a year after the collapse of the World Trade Center on September 11, 2001, PeaceWalk 2002 manifested the resolve of participants to continue working for a better world. Buddhist participants purchased land for a retreat center, Magnolia Village in northern Mississippi. In 2005, Nhat Hanh returned for a formal dedication.

These experiences with Nhat Hanh renewed my conviction that each of us is custodian of tremendous energy for transformation of our own being, and the lives of others. We can change the way we think, speak, or act and become the stone that, thrown into a body of water, ripples outward.

Each of the three spiritual masters, among many others, have taught me to live contemplatively in a world of action. Death prematurely took

---

the Beloved Community: A Journey with the Fellowship of Reconciliation (2005) and *Dangerous People: The Fellowship of Reconciliation Building a Nonviolent World of Justice, Peace, and Freedom* (2016).

the lives of two. At the time of writing, the third, Nhat Hanh, remained active and able to return on a mission of reconciliation to Vietnam. I learned with sadness that he died on October 6, 2020. The witness of each encourages us to claim the power of silence, compassion, and love in our own lives as we work to realize the Beloved Community, Dr. King's phrase for the reign of God.

9

Merton on Gandhi

THOMAS MERTON WAS A student at Oakham, a British coeducational independent school, when, in late 1931, the second London Round Table
Conference met to explore a future for India.[1] Merton recalled arguing
about Gandhi in his school dormitory, chiefly against the football captain who called British rule benevolent, a civilizing enterprise for which
Indians were not suitably grateful. The "complacent idiocy of this argument" infuriated Merton who thought, "Such sentiments were of course
beyond comprehension. How could Gandhi be right when he was *odd*?
And how could I be right if I was on the side of someone who had the
wrong kind of skin, and left altogether too much of it exposed?" Merton
thought that the millions of people who lived in India were perfectly justi-
fied in demanding that the British withdraw peacefully and allow them
to run their own country." In 1947, "the British Empire collapsed. India
attained self-rule. It did so peacefully and with dignity. Gandhi paid with
his life for the ideals which he believed."[2]

At the time Merton may not have known Gandhian principles like
ahimsa (nonviolent resistance), *swadeshi* (self-reliance), or *satyagraha*
(truth force). However, Merton was developing a Gandhi-like aversion to
war. As early as June 16, 1940, Merton journaled,

> I don't pretend, like other people, to understand the war [World
> War II], I do know this much: that the knowledge of what is
> going on only makes it seem desperately important to be

1. See Dekar, "Thomas Merton, Gandhi"; Dekar, "Thomas Merton on Gandhi and
Nonviolence"; and Dekar, *Thomas Merton: Twentieth-Century Wisdom*, 141–50. Gandhi's *Autobiography* and Fischer's *Life of Mahatma Gandhi* offer background for the
1982 Academy Award-winning film *Gandhi*. Gandhi, *All Men Are Brothers*, 181–84, has
a brief chronology of key events in Gandhi's life.

2. Merton, *Seeds of Destruction*, 222–23, Merton's emphasis.

voluntarily poor, to get rid of all possessions this instant. I am scared, sometimes, to own anything, even a name, let alone a coin, or shares in the oil, the munitions, the airplane factories. I am scared to take a proprietary interest in anything, for fear that my love of what I own may be killing somebody somewhere.[3]

Over the next few years, Gandhi's name appeared occasionally in Merton's writing. For example, in an October 10, 1960, journal entry, Merton mentioned how he needed to understand Gandhi and practice nonviolence in every way.[4] On May 31, 1961, Merton noted,

Gandhi once asked, "How can he who thinks he possesses absolute truth be fraternal?" Let us be frank about it: the history of Christianity raises the question again and again. Doubtless Gandhi implies an answer that is too simple and leads to vague indifferentism. The problem: God has revealed Himself as love first of all. But this is inseparable from the truth of the gospel message. Only he who loves has really grasped the truth of the message.[5]

In 1964, Merton wrote two essays on Gandhi. "A Tribute to Gandhi" appeared in Seeds of Destruction.[6] "Gandhi and the One-Eyed Giant" introduced Gandhi on Nonviolence: A Selection from the Writings of Mahatma Gandhi. Merton wrote other books reflective of his interest in Asia: The Way of Chuang Tzu (1965); Mystics and Zen Masters (1967); Zen and the Birds of Appetite (1968); and The Asian Journal, published posthumously.[7]

In his tribute to Gandhi, "the gentle revolutionary," Merton recalled his earlier defense of Gandhi and observed that events had overtaken Europe "with greater violence and more unmitigated fury than all that had ever been attributed by the wildest imaginations to the despots of Asia. The British empire collapsed. India attained self-rule. It did so peacefully and with dignity. Gandhi paid with his life for the ideals in which he believed." Merton contrasted Gandhi favorably with all other world figures of the time:

---

3. Merton, Run to the Mountain, 231–32, entry for June 16, 1940.

4. Merton, Turning toward the World, 57.

5. Merton, Turning toward the World, 122–23.

6. See "Tribute to Gandhi" in Merton, Seeds of Destruction, 221–34; reprinted in the December 1964 issue of Ramparts, a Catholic periodical, and as "Gandhi: The Gentle Revolutionary," in Merton, Passion for Peace, 202–9.

7. Merton mentioned Gandhi in Conjectures of a Guilty Bystander (1966). In "Seven Lessons for Inter-faith Dialogue," Allan M. McMillan attributed Merton's burst of writing on world religions to his prayer life, his self-examination, and his desire to grow through shared experiences with others on a similar quest.

[Gandhi was] an extraordinary leader of men . . . radically different from the others . . . remains in our time as a sign of the
genuine union of spiritual fervor and social action in the midst
of a hundred pseudo-spiritual cryptofascist, or communist movements in which the capacity for creative and spontaneous dedication is captured, debased and exploited by the false prophets.[8]

Acknowledging that Gandhi was not above criticism, Merton stressed
that, unlike other world leaders of his day, Gandhi lived in a manner marked
"by a wholeness and a wisdom, an integrity and a spiritual consistency that
the others lacked, or manifested only in reverse, in consistent fidelity to a
dynamism of evil and destruction." Merton emphasized, "His [Gandhi's]
way was no secret: it was simply to follow conscience without regard for
the consequences to himself, in the belief that this was demanded of him
by God and that the results would be the work of God. Perhaps indeed for a
long time these results would remain hidden as God's secret. But in the end
the truth would manifest itself."[9]

Merton contended that Gandhi recognized the impossibility of being peaceful or nonviolent if one is controlled by the "insatiable requirements of a society maddened by overstimulation and obsessed with the
demons of noise, voyeurism and speed." Gandhi recalled that Jesus taught
his followers to regulate the whole of life by the "eternal law of love," the
acceptance of which "had been made known to the world in traditional
religions and most clearly by Jesus Christ." For Merton, Gandhi's whole life
including his activism and death "were nothing but a witness to this commitment: "IF LOVE IS NOT THE LAW OF OUR BEING THE WHOLE
OF MY ARGUMENT FALLS TO PIECES."[10]

Merton understood that Gandhi expressly dissociated himself from
Christianity as an institution. But Gandhi built his whole life and all his
activity upon what he regarded the law of Christ. Merton stressed Gandhi's
commitment to nonviolence and observance of spiritual disciplines like
fasting, observing days of silence, and retreats. Gandhi was generous in
listening to and communicating with others. Merton thought that he, like
Gandhi, could not be a peaceful, nonviolent person by submitting passively to the insatiable requirements of a culture maddened by overstimulation, violence, lust, and greed.

8. Merton, *Passion for Peace*, 203, 206.

9. Merton, *Passion for Peace*, 204.

10. Merton, *Passion for Peace*, 209, Merton's emphasis. In *Gandhi on Non-Violence*,
Merton repeats this with slightly different wording: "If love or non-violence be not the
law of our being, the whole of my argument falls to pieces" (25).

In short, Merton saw Gandhi as offering a "model of integrity whom we cannot afford to ignore, and the one basic duty we all owe to the world, to imitate him in 'dissociating ourselves from evil in total disregard of the consequences." Merton concluded this essay, "May God mercifully grant us the grace to be half as sincere and half as generous as was this great leader, one of the noblest men of our century."[11]

Writing in his journal entry for November 22, 1960, Merton mentioned his struggle with Abbot Fox.[12] Fox warned Merton about "not having contact with the world," including several who were "working for a more intelligent and living form of monasticism." Among examples, Merton mentioned Bede Griffiths (1906–93), an English Benedictine who founded in India a Christian community that adopted Hindu ways of life and thought, and Jean Leclercq (1911–93), a French Benedictine who subsequently invited Merton to a Buddhist-Christian monastic retreat in Thailand where Merton died. Merton interpreted Fox's ban as a "deliberate policy of stifling real aspirations and substituting conformity to the policies of confused, inert, businesslike, middle-class monasticism which is ours." Mentioning he was gathering texts on Gandhian nonviolence, Merton continued:

> Sense of obscure struggle to find a genuinely true and honest position in the world and its belligerent affairs. I wish I knew where to stand. I think I stand with a Gandhi more than with anyone else. But how to transpose his principles to suit my own situation? . . . A growing obscure conviction that this country, having been weighted in the balance and found wanting, faces a dreadful judgment.
>
> Yet I am always ready to feel this and don't know how to interpret such ideas after all. The whole world is judged.[13]

Merton's second essay, "Gandhi and the One-Eyed Giant," introduced an entry-level selection of quotes from Gandhi's *Gandhi on Non-Violence*. Merton attributed the "one-eye giant" phrase to Laurens van der Post (1906–96), a South African Afrikaner to whom Merton dedicated *The Behavior of Titans*.

> See the important book, *The Dark Eye in Africa*, with its thesis that the white man's spiritual rejection and contempt for the

---

11. Merton, *Passion for Peace*, 209.

12. See Lucas, *Merton's Abbot*; Quenon, Review of *Merton's Abbot*; and Shannon's entry in *Thomas Merton Encyclopedia*, 160–61. Despite their sometimes strained relationship, Merton and Fox are buried next to each other. For a photo, see https://www.flickr.com/photos/jimforest/5082471505/.

13. Merton, *Turning toward the World*, 68–69.

African is the result of his rejection of what is deepest and most vital in himself. Having "lost his own soul," the materialistic and cunning exploiter of the colonies destroyed the soul of the native. The "one-eyed giant" has "outer vision" only, no "inner vision." Therefore, though he tries to take precautions to avoid spiritual disaster for himself and the races he has subjugated, these precautions are "without perspective" and in "the wrong dimension of reality."[14]

For Merton, the one-eyed giant manifested a "characteristic split and blindness which were at once his strength, his torment, and his ruin . . . . The one-eyed had science without wisdom." Westerners had lost all that made life sacred and meaningful. Merton thought, "Neither the ancient wisdoms nor the modern sciences are complete in themselves. They do not stand alone. They call for one another."[15] Merton affirmed the value arising from the potential union of ancient wisdom and modern science, a marriage that "was wrecked on the rocks of the white man's dualism and of the inertia, the incomprehension, of ancient and primitive societies." Nevertheless, a new age, post-modern (and perhaps post historical) was dawning. Merton believed that "the spiritual consciousness of a people awakened in the spirit of one person. But the message . . . was not for India alone. It was for the whole world. Hence Gandhi's message was valid for India and for himself in so far as it represented *the awakening of a new world*."[16]

Early in his life, Gandhi spoke, thought, and acted as an Englishman. He was an "alienated Asian . . . betraying his own heritage and his own self, thinking as a white man without ceasing to be 'a Nigger.'"[17] This resulted from his British education in South Africa and England.

Merton considered Gandhi's recovery of the Hindu roots of Indian culture significant. Gandhi considered Hindu concepts as having universal significance, including *dharma* (duty), *ahimsa* (nonviolent resistance),

14. In a footnote to his essay, "Gandhi and the One-Eyed Giant" Merton cites a *New York Times* reviewer of Van der Post's book characterized it as having "the timelessness of true philosophy, but today's world situation gives them a special urgency. Every cultured mind or student of Africa interested in its emergence as a world force should read *The Dark Eye in Africa*. 'If you fail to read it, you will miss one of the most fascinating and profound statements to come out of Africa on the subject of man's bitter war against himself.'" In *The Lost World of the Kalahari*, in a chapter entitled "The Vanished People," van der Post refers to "the obscene intent which some European archaeologists have projected into him [the Bushman]" (8).

15. Merton, *Gandhi on Non-Violence*, 1.

16. Merton, *Gandhi on Non-Violence*, 5.

17. Merton, *Gandhi on Non-Violence*, 3.

and *satyagraha* (truth force). Gandhi never creased to value the wisdom of teachers from other religious tradition.

In section 1 of the anthology, "Principles of Non-violence," Gandhi identified "non-violence" not as a garment to be put on and off at will, but rather "the heart . . . an inseparable part of our being."[18] Gandhi lifted up Jesus, a supreme practitioner of love, foundational to a nonviolent lifestyle. "Jesus lived and died in vain if He did not teach us to regulate the whole of life by the eternal law of love."[19]

In section 2, "Non-violence: True and False," Gandhi again referred to Jesus, who he characterized "as the most active resister known perhaps to history. This was non-violence par excellence."[20]

What specifically did Merton consider Gandhi's contribution to the theory and practice of nonviolence? One was the rejection of an imposed identity in favor of "inner unity which is *the fruit of inner unity already achieved.*"[21] Another was Gandhi's understanding that the spiritual or interior life is not an exclusively private affair. One of the marks of a *satyagrahi*, a seeker of truth, was that, as a person deepens his or her inner life, he or she necessarily enters into a deeper understanding of and communion with the spirit of other people.

Merton concluded that, although Gandhi's career was eminently active rather than contemplative, Gandhi was faithful "in maintaining intact the contemplative element that is necessary in every life . . . even his days of silence and retirement were not days of mere 'privacy'; they belonged to India and he owed them to India, because his 'spiritual life' was simply his participation in the life and *dharma* of his people."[22]

A third key idea was that of justice. Citing Gandhi, Merton continued:

> "Hinduism excludes all exploitation" (hence it follows implicitly that the caste structure in so far as it rested upon a basis of crass injustice toward the *Harijan* [untouchables, described by Gandhi as beautiful people] was in fact a denial of the basic truth of Hinduism). Gandhi's sense of the Hindu *dharma* demanded, then, that this be made clear and that all Hindus should collaborate in setting things right. This fundamental re-establishment of justice was essential if India was to have the inner unity, strength, and freedom to profit by its own political liberation.[23]

18. Merton, *Gandhi on Non-Violence*, 24.
19. Merton, *Gandhi on Non-Violence*, 26.
20. Merton, *Gandhi on Non-Violence*, 40.
21. Merton, *Gandhi on Non-Violence*, 6, Merton's emphasis.
22. Merton, *Gandhi on Non-Violence*, 7.
23. Merton, *Gandhi on Non-Violence*, 9.

Merton recognized Gandhi did not identify the private sphere with the sacred, nor did he cut himself off from public activity as secular. In the end, he could not impose his abhorrence of the caste system upon newly independent India and was in fact assassinated by a Hindu fanatic.

A fourth key idea was that of *satyagraha*, or truth force. Merton wrote, "Sometimes the idea of nonviolence is taken to be the result of a purely sentimental evasion of unpleasant reality. Foggy clichés about Oriental metaphysics leave complacent Westerners with the idea that . . . Easterners are all 'quietists.'"[24]

Merton rejected such thinking and understood Gandhi as having demonstrated that nonviolent action was not merely a means by which the weak could come to power, but a way of being. By changing his life and seeking to live in a nonviolent manner, Gandhi became a model for *satyagrahi* to exercise power through love and truth. In short, nonviolence was not something passive but a noble and effective way to express love and defend rights. Not merely a private affair, *ahimsa* required that all means of all political action be consistent with desired results.

Gandhi did not expect everyone to live perfectly but believed that, given proper training and proper generalship, the masses could practice nonviolence. Writing that "*Non-violence is the supreme law*" Gandhi observed that during his half a century of experience, "I have not yet come across a situation when I had to say that I was helpless, that I had no remedy in terms of non-violence."[25]

One area to which Gandhi applied his theory concerned the future of the British mandate over Palestine, and the emerging Jewish-Arab conflict that has erupted in intermittent wars since 1948. In a November 26, 1938, article in the weekly *Harijan*, Gandhi wrote, "Palestine belongs to the Arabs in the same sense that England belongs to the English."[26]

Major Jewish voices like philosopher Martin Buber (1878–1965) and Judah Magnes (1877–1948), first President of Hebrew University in Jerusalem, wrote Gandhi, insisting that he was ignoring the gravity of Nazism. Gandhi did not reply to either and reportedly told his biographer, Louis Fischer, that "Judaism is obstinate and unenlightened."[27]

---

24. Merton, *Gandhi on Non-Violence*, 11.

25. Merton, *Gandhi on Non-Violence*, 25, Gandhi's emphasis.

26. Mendes-Flohr, *Land of Two Peoples*, 108, and the following articles by Dekar: "Christians, Jews and the Holy Land"; "Does the State of Israel Have Theological Significance?"; "The Peace Movement in Israel"; and "Gandhi, Satyagraha, and the Israel-Palestine Conflict."

27. Shimoni, *Gandhi, Satyagraha and the Jews*, 19.

In compiling selections from Gandhi's book, Merton did not address the controversy generated by Gandhi's views on the Holy Land. Merton did focus on extraordinary means needed to sustain nonviolent life ways. Merton highlighted the supernatural valor available through spiritual practices such as prayer and meditation. Courage demanded nothing short of the ability to face death with complete fearlessness and to suffer without retaliation. Nonviolence was meaningless without spiritual practice. As he urged Jim Forest, at the time a Catholic Peace Fellowship activist,

> Do not depend on the hope of results. When you are doing the sort of work you have taken on, essentially an apostolic work, you may have to face the fact that your work will be apparently worthless and even achieve no result at all . . . just serve Christ's truth [and believe] God is making something good . . . in some way we cannot see.[28]

Merton organized the selection of quotes from Gandhi's *Gandhi on Non-Violence* in five sections. The first, "Principles of Non-violence," introduced *ahimsa*, nonviolence, as "the only true force in life" and "the supreme law."[29] In this section, Merton included quotes on an issue about which he was especially passionate—nuclear weapons:

> So far as I can see, the atomic bomb has deadened the finest feeling that has sustained mankind for ages. There used to be the so-called laws of war which made it tolerable. Now we know the naked truth. War knows no law except that of might. The atom bomb brought an empty victory to the allied arms, but it resulted for the time being in destroying the soul of Japan. What has happened to the soul of the destroying nation is yet too early to see.
>
> Mankind has to get out of violence only through nonviolence. Hatred can be overcome only by love. Counter-hatred only increases the surface as well as the depth of hatred.
>
> I regard the employment of the atom bomb for the wholesale destruction of men, women and children as the most diabolical use of science.[30]

Introducing the second section, "Non-violence: True and False," Merton highlighted nonviolence as a charismatic gift, a creed, and a passion for which one sacrifices everything, a complete way of life in which

28. On February 21, 1966, Merton responded to Forest's request for "some thoughts that would help." Merton, *Essential Writings*, 136.

29. Gandhi, *Gandhi on Non-Violence*, 25.

30. Gandhi, *Gandhi on Non-Violence*, 32.

the satyagrahi is totally dedicated to the transformation of his own life, adversaries, and society by means of love. Merton observed that Gandhi believed nonviolence to be "the noblest as well as the most effective way of defending one's rights."[31]

The third section emphasized the spiritual dimension of nonviolence. In his introduction, Merton wrote that Gandhi believes nonviolence to be more natural than violence, an inherent disposition to love. Believing a truly free and just society must be constructed on a foundation of nonviolence, Merton cited Gandhi as critical of Western democracy as it functioned at the time as "diluted nazism or fascism."[32]

Selections in the fourth section explored the political scope of nonviolence. Merton stressed that Gandhi embraced all of life in a consistent and logical network of obligations. Merton addressed the threat of nuclear annihilation and the need to build a world at peace on the basis of inclusivity and tolerance. "There is no escape for any of us save through truth and non-violence. I know that war is wrong, is an unmitigated evil. I know too that it has got to go. I firmly believe that freedom won through bloodshed or fraud is no freedom."[33]

In the final section, "The Purity of Non-violence," Merton summarized five key elements needed to act nonviolently:

1.   It implies not wishing ill.

2.   It includes total refusal to cooperate with or participate in activities of the unjust group, even to eating food coming from them.

3.   It is of no avail to those without living faith in the God of love and love for all mankind.

4.   He who practices it must be ready to sacrifice everything except his honor.

5.   It must pervade *everything* and not be applied merely to isolated acts.[34]

Drawing on his experience with an ambulance unit in South Africa during the Boer War, Gandhi called for formation of a nonviolent volunteer corps, or peace brigades that would interpose in situations of violent conflict. Peace brigaders were to observe several rules. They may not carry

31. Merton, introduction to Section Two, in Gandhi, *Gandhi on Non-Violence*, 35.
32. Merton, introduction to Section Three, in Gandhi, *Gandhi on Non-Violence*, 45.
33. Gandhi, *Gandhi on Non-Violence*, 52.
34. Gandhi, *Gandhi on Non-Violence*, 64, Gandhi's emphasis.

any weapons. They must be easily recognizable. They must carry supplies and know how to render first aid. They should know how to put out fires. They should be well acquainted with residents of the locality. And they should pray. In an article in *Harijan*, Gandhi elaborated what was expected of such "messengers of peace":

> If the Congress is to succeed in its non-violent struggle, it must develop the power to deal peacefully with such situations. Let us therefore see what qualifications a member of the contemplated Peace Brigade should possess. He or she must have a living faith in non-violence. This is impossible without a living faith in God. A non-violent man can do nothing save by the power and grace of God. Without it he won't have the courage to die without anger, without fear and without retaliation. Such courage comes from the belief that God sits in the hearts of all and that there should be no fear in the presence of God. The knowledge of the omnipresence of God also means respect for the lives of even those who may be called opponents or goondas. . . .
>
> This messenger of peace must have equal regard for all the principal religions of the earth. Thus if he is a Hindu, he will respect the other faiths current in India. He must therefore possess a knowledge of the general principles of the different faiths professed in the country . . . . The work can be done singly or in groups. Therefore no one need wait for companions. Nevertheless one would naturally seek companions in one's own locality and form a local Brigade.
>
> This messenger of peace will cultivate through personal service contacts with the people in his locality or chosen circle, so that when he appears to deal with ugly situations, he does not descend upon the members of a riotous assembly as an utter stranger liable to be looked upon as a suspect or an unwelcome visitor.[35]

Merton's selection of Gandhi quotes had wide influence. Merton sent the book to diverse individuals, including musician Joan Baez who visited Merton on December 10, 1966. Merton described the day as "memorable.[36] In an earlier entry, Merton mentioned borrowing her records from Father Chrysogonus (especially "Silver Dollar") and music of Bob Dylan.[37]

---

35. Gandhi, *Gandhi on Non-Violence*, 71; see also *Harijan*, 18-6-38 at https://www.gandhiashramsevagram.org/my-dream-india/chapter-69-peace-brigades.php.

36. Merton, *Learning to Love*, 167.

37. Merton, *Learning to Love*, 83, entry for June 14, 1966.

Merton also sent his Gandhi collection to members of the Student Nonviolent Coordinating Committee, one of several civil rights organizations active in the 1960s; Catholic Sister M. Emmanuel de Souza e Silva, who worked in the slums of Rio de Janeiro; participants in the 1964 peacemakers retreat at Gethsemani; and James Douglass, a Catholic in the anti-nuclear movement and the author of a book on Gandhi in which Douglass refers to Merton's essays on Gandhi.[38]

On July 14, 1965, Douglass and his wife Shelly visited Merton. Journaling, Merton reflected on the "stupidity" of the Vietnam War "in a way that everyone can see except the average American! Jim says polls are running 70% in favor of the war . . . . A fiction of self-generating public opinion, which justifies everything."[39]

On November 7, Douglass wrote Merton and enclosed a clipping about Roger Laporte who burned himself in front of the Pentagon in protest of the Vietnam War. Merton mused that some would try to write him off as a nut, "but he seems to have been a perfectly responsible person, a Quaker, very dedicated. . . . I do not know that his motives were necessarily wrong or confused—all I can say is that objectively it is a terrible thing. . . . O God, what a tragic world we live in! Meanwhile the Catholic Workers are all burning their draft cards."[40]

Distressed by Laporte's suicide and the expanding Vietnam conflict, Merton sent telegrams to Dorothy Day and James Forest. Merton indicated he could no longer support the Catholic Peace Fellowship or its parent body, the Fellowship of Reconciliation, a judgement he subsequently reversed.

Gandhi's call to form "local brigades" inspired civil society organizations such as Peace Brigades International, Nonviolence Peace Force, and FOR. The latter has maintained a peace presence in the community of San José de Apartadó, Colombia, with a field team of two to three members who have supported coffee workers throughout the of civil conflict.

In 2009, I participated in a "peace brigade" to visit that work in Colombia. As I departed, my wife asked if I could die. I knew that members of the military had killed villagers who were in effect collateral damage in the wider conflict. I replied to Nancy, "Yes." However, I reassured her that it was highly unlikely either side in the conflict would risk attracting international scrutiny in the event of the death of a nonviolent peace worker.[41]

38. Douglass, *Gandhi and the Unspeakable*, xii–xiii. In July 1993, I spent some time with Douglass in Birmingham, Alabama, where he and his wife Shelly have established Mary's House, part of the Catholic Worker network.

39. Merton, *Dancing in the Water of Life*, 270.

40. Merton, *Dancing in the Water of Life*, 313.

41. See my "Swadeshi in Colombia," 14–15. My books *Creating the Beloved*

Gandhi's influence on Merton's thinking was manifest at a retreat on the "spiritual roots of protest" at the Abbey of Our Lady of Gethsemani in November 1964.[42] Proposed by FOR, Merton took a lead role as host at the site of his future hermitage. Participants included a Mennonite theologian John Howard Yoder; A. J. Muste, former executive director of the FOR, and John Oliver Nelson, onetime national FOR chairperson. Catholic participants included Dan Berrigan, Phil Berrigan, John Peter Grady, Tom Cornell and Jim Forest, who with Cornell was then involved with the Catholic Peace Fellowship. Merton began by explaining the purpose of the gathering, as follows:

> We are hoping to reflect together during these days on our common grounds for religious dissent and commitment in the face of the injustice and disorder of a world in which total war seems at times inevitable, in which few seek any but violent solutions to economic and social problems more critical and more vast than man has ever known.

Merton asked, "By what right do we assume that we are called to protest, to judge, and to witness?" and affirmed that people protest because "within me there is something like a burning fire shut up in my bones; I am weary with holding it in, and I cannot" (Jer 20:9). Merton went on by calling for the building of a new sacral order, a millennial "city" in which God is manifest and praised by free and enlightened people.

Merton prayed that this latter outcome might emerge. He did not believe at the time that technology was morally or religiously promising. "Does this call for reaction and protest; if so, what kind? What can we really do about it?" As a partial response, Merton called for *metanoia*. By this Greek word, he did not mean conversion, as translators often misinterpret. Merton had in mind total personal transformation and fidelity to monastic life. Merton called for a radical turn to the gospel of peace. People must sacrifice, suffer, and participate in redemptive protest. Expecting "the future will depend on what we do in the present," Merton read excerpts from his Gandhi anthology.

Community and *Dangerous People* provide a history of FOR and affiliates like Catholic Peace Fellowship in the U.S. For other organizations, see https://www.peacebrigades. org; www.ifor.org; and https://www.nonviolentpeaceforce.org.

42. Oyer, *Pursuing the Spiritual Roots of Protest*. In addition to myself, Bill Apel, Deborah Belcasstro, Gordon Oyer, and Patricia Schnapp had an excellent discussion as a symposium; see *Merton Annual* 28 (2015) 215–38. One of the retreatants, Tom Cornell, reviewed *Thomas Merton on Peace*, ed. Gordon C. Zahn, in *Fellowship* 40 (January 1974) 23.

In "Blessed Are the Meek: The Christian Roots of Nonviolence," reprinted in various formats, Merton summarized Gandhian principles of nonviolence:

1. "Nonviolence must be aimed above all at the transformation of the present state of the world." People must live nonviolently. For Merton, followers of Jesus should manifest the ethic of Christ through living a way of life without necessarily becoming political. Merton cautioned against being drawn into power struggles or identifying too much with one side or another of a conflict.

2. "The nonviolent resistance of the Christian who belongs to one of the powerful nations and who is himself in some sense a privileged member of world society will have to be clearly for others, that is, for the poor and underprivileged." Merton cited the struggle of African American civil rights activists as exemplars of *ahimsa* and *satyagraha*.

3. "In the case of nonviolent struggle for peace—the threat of nuclear war abolishes all privileges." Especially during the 1960s, Merton wrote against nuclear weaponry.

4. "Perhaps the most insidious temptation to be avoided is one which is characteristic of the power structure itself: this fetishism of immediate visible results." As a spiritual director to activists, Merton cautioned against depending on results. The work of the peacemaker is essentially an expression of humility.

5. "Christian nonviolence is convinced that the manner in which the conflict for truth is waged will itself manifest or obscure the truth. To fight for truth by dishonest, violent, inhuman, or unreasonable means would simply betray the truth one is trying to vindicate." Merton did not support some measures of anti-war activists, such as self-immolation or burning draft records.

6. "A test of our sincerity . . . is this: are we willing to learn something from the adversary? . . . Are we willing to admit that the adversary is not totally inhumane, wrong, unreasonable, cruel, etc.? . . . Nonviolence has great power, provided that it really witnesses to truth and not just to self-righteousness." Believing that contestants on any side of any dispute have rights, Merton insisted in seeing some good in those who disagreed with him and in affirming some of their ideas. Being open-minded towards the views of others, a nonviolent resister discovers one's own truth in a new light.

7. "Christian hope and Christian humility are inseparable. The quality of nonviolence is decided largely by the purity of the Christian hope behind it."[43]

Throughout his life, Merton referred to Gandhi and Hinduism. In *The Seven Storey Mountain*, Merton mentioned reading the *Spiritual Exercises* of Ignatius of Loyola, founder of the Society of Jesus. Merton thought that Jesuits would have had "a nasty shock if they had walked in and seen me doing their *Spiritual Exercises* sitting there like Mahatma Gandhi."[44] That such a positive reference to a non-Christian made it past the scrutiny of Merton's censors was significant, foretelling Merton's ability to look deeper and to dialogue honestly with adherents of non-Christian religions.

In *Conjectures of a Guilty Bystander*, Merton mentioned Gandhi several times. In urging war resistance, Merton cited Gandhi, who wrote, according to Roman Rolland,

"To refuse military service when the time has come for it to be necessary, is to act *after* the time to combat the evil has run out." Compulsory military service is only a symptom of a deeper evil. All who support the state in its organizing for war or in policies that imply the willingness to organize for war, and all who profit by privileges in such a state, have no business refusing military service. The refusal must be much more radical and much more sacrificial. It implies the refusal of privileges and benefits as well as of cooperation in a few policies with which one does not agree.[45]

In Part Two, "Truth and Violence: An Interesting Era," Merton reflected at length on Gandhi's conviction that Western democracy was on trial.

Gandhi saw that Western democracy was on trial. On trial for what? On trial to be judged by its own claims to be the rule of the people by themselves. Not realizing itself to be on trial, assuming its own infallibility and perfection, Western democracy has resented every attempt to question these things The mere idea that it might come under judgment has seemed absurd, unjust, diabolical. Our democracy is now being judged. not by man but by God. . . .

Democracy has been on trial in Berlin, in Alabama, in Hiroshima, in World War II, in World War I, in the Boer War [where Gandhi first developed his key principles]. In the

43. Merton, *Passion for Peace*, 248–59; Merton, *Words of Peace*, 17–22.

44. Merton, *Seven Storey Mountain*, 269. For a contemporary translation by Anthony Mottola, see Ignatius, *Spiritual Exercises of St. Ignatius* (1964).

45. Merton, *Conjectures of a Guilty Bystander*, 54–55.

American Civil War. In the Opium War. What have we learned about ourselves? What have we seen? What have we admitted? What is the truth about us? Perhaps we still have time, still have a little light to see by. But the judgment is getting very dark. The truth is too enormous, too ominous, to be seen in comfort. Yet it is a great mercy of God that so many of us can recognize this fact, and that we are still allowed to *say* it.[46]

Again in *Conjectures of a Guilty Bystander*, Merton quoted Gandhi's *My Non-violence*:

"The business of every God-fearing man," says Gandhi, "is to dissociate himself from evil in *total disregard of the consequences*. He must have faith in a good deed producing only a good result . . . He follows the truth though the following of it may endanger his very life. He knows that it is better to die in the way of God than to live in the way of Satan."

Merton commented, "This is precisely the attitude that we have lost in the West, because we have lost our fundamentally religious view of reality, of being and of truth. And this is what Gandhi retained. We have sacrificed the power to apprehend and respect what man is, what truth is, what love is, and have replaced them with a vague confusion of pragmatic notions."[47]

Merton stressed that reliance on God did not mean passivity. On the contrary, it freed people for a clearly defined activity—"the will of God," in Gandhi's words, "intelligent action in a detached manner." For Merton, this was the "law of love."[48]

In 1968, Merton traveled to India where he met disciples of Gandhi. In the journal of his Asian journey, Merton often mentioned Gandhi. On November 19, 1968, writing while he was in Calcutta, Merton reflected on the tragic circumstances of Gandhi's death. On January 30, 1948, a member of an extremist Hindu party murdered Gandhi. Merton wrote, "Gandhi's nonviolence was not a sentimental evasion or denial of the reality of evil. It was a clear-sighted acceptance of the necessity to use the force and the presence of evil as a fulcrum for good and for liberation."[49]

During his India pilgrimage, Merton demonstrated a deep engagement with the living faiths of Asia. Having come to believe that the contemplative life could not be merely a turning of one's back on the world, Merton had

---

46. Merton, *Conjectures of a Guilty Bystander*, 80.

47. Merton, *Conjectures of a Guilty Bystander*, 117.

48. Merton, *Conjectures of a Guilty Bystander*, 120.

49. Merton, "Gandhi and the One-Eyed Giant," 11.

assumed a new calling, that of a prophet for people seeking to bring into being a new world of greater understanding of and respect for all religions.

In 1996, McMaster University established an annual Mahatma Gandhi Lectureship under the direction of the Centre for Peace Studies.[50] These lectures have sought to make the value and strategies of nonviolence widely known, and to develop the concept and practice of nonviolence through intellectual analysis and criticism, dialogue, debate, and experimentation. The series has played a role in the revitalization and development of nonviolence. Gandhi brought together East and West, spirituality and practical politics, the ancient and the contemporary, and in so doing he helped rescue ensure that Gandhi is not put on a pedestal, but rather taken seriously.

This Gandhian perspective was manifest on November 1–7, 2018, in Toronto, Canada, during the Parliament of the World's Religions, which met under the theme, "Inclusion, the Power of Love: Pursuing Global Understanding, Reconciliation and Change." An estimated six to eight thousand adherents of virtually every region and religion, including pagan groups, gathered. Several speakers, including Gandhi's grandson Arun Gandhi, encouraged participants to follow Mahatma Gandhi in expressing spirituality in all of life. The range of exhibits, films, issues, music, speakers, storytelling, and workshops was extraordinary. Plenaries each morning and evening featured noted speakers and musicians. Each afternoon, concurrent workshops and interest groups highlighted ways to express spirituality without formal institutional grounding. A local paper characterized the gathering as "a microcosm of how the world could be."[51]

As I have researched and written this chapter, I have rediscovered the writings of Merton on Gandhi as having deep, ongoing importance. On three occasions I have traveled through India. In some ways, Gandhiji [the affectionate popular name most people in India use to refer to Gandhi] is

---

50. "Mahatma Gandhi Lectures on Nonviolence."

51. Friessen, "Parliment of the World's Religions Conference," A8. I wrote a report for my Quaker community in which I provided background. In 1893 in Chicago, Illinois, some four thousand individuals attended the first Parliament of World Religions, held in conjunction with the World's Columbian Exhibition. In 1993, some eight thousand individuals attended, again in Chicago, a centennial gathering generating Towards a Global Ethic, a powerful statement of the ethical common ground shared by the world's religions and spiritual traditions. Subsequently, there have been Parliaments of the World Religions in Cape Town, South Africa (1999); Barcelona, Spain (2004); Melbourne, Australia (2009); Salt Lake City, USA (2015) and Toronto (November 1–7, 2018). The movement's goal has been and remains the cultivation of harmony among global religious and spiritual communities to build a more just, peaceful, and sustainable world. The theme of the Toronto gathering was "The Promise of Inclusion, the Power of Love: Pursuing Global Understanding, Reconciliation and Change."

more revered as father of the nation, than followed. Nonetheless, I also met people who are his true successors.

We live in a culture that not only accepts but often celebrates and encourages violence in its many forms to solve our problems. While it might be easy to blame elected officials, with notable exceptions they are symptoms, not causes, of a wider problem—specifically, acceptance of violence as a means to pursue goals, however legitimate. Only by delegitimating violence will politicians cease to feel the pressure or sanction to seek to resolve disputes nonviolently. Only when we have mainstreamed nonviolence can we begin to deepen the unfolding of the dream of Merton, truly God's messenger envisioning a new world of justice, peace, integrity of creation, and interdependence. Like Gandhi and Martin Luther King Jr., Merton dreamed of a different world than that which characterized his time. In a world dominated by science, technology, the drive to acquire power for its own sake, materialism, and consumerism, we need to hear their voices and walk the talk.

10

Thomas Merton's Embrace of "the Other" Reflected in Letters with Ernesto Cardenal

So then you are no longer strangers and aliens, but you are citizens with the saints and also members of the household of God, built upon the foundation of the apostles and prophets, with Christ Jesus himself as the cornerstone.

—Ephesians 2:19–20

Let me be quite succinct: the greatest sin of the European-Russian-American complex that we call "the West" . . . is not only greed and cruelty, not only moral dishonesty and infidelity to truth, but above all *its unmitigated arrogance toward the rest of the human race*.[1]

IN THE 1950S AND 1960S, Thomas Merton—a white man living in the South—was ahead of his time in analyzing structures that sustained racism and in acknowledging his duty and the responsibility of all Christians to discern truth in what people of color called for in liberation struggles. In this chapter, I explore Merton's embrace of "the other" with attention to letters to and from Ernesto Cardenal (1925–2020), onetime novice at Gethsemani. In 1984, Pope John Paul II suspended Cardenal from some priestly duties because of his theology of liberation and for serving as minister of culture from 1979 to 1987 in the government of Daniel Ortega, who took power in 1979.

---

1. Merton, *From the Monastery to the World*, 267–68. A Spanish-language edition was published in 1998. See Merton, *Collected Poems of Thomas Merton*, 849–55, for selections from Cardenal's *Gethsemani, Ky.*

Christine Bochen and others have reviewed Merton's and Cardenal's letters.[2] However, the decision of Pope Francis in 2019 to lift sanctions on Cardenal, and the latter's death in early 2020, invite fresh consideration of the Merton-Cardenal correspondence.[3]

Cardenal was born in Granada, Nicaragua, to an upper-middle-class family at a time when US marines occupied his country, allegedly to protect US commercial activity. He was raised in León. The city was noted for resistance to US imperialism. León was the home of the poet Rubén Dario (1867–1916), who criticized the United States. It was also a center of support for Augusto Sandino (1895–1934), who emerged as guerrilla war leader against General Anastasio Somoza García (1896–1956). Somoza had seized power in 1934 and established a dictatorship that ruled Nicaragua for more than forty years with US support.

Cardenal completed his primary and secondary education in Nicaragua. He then studied literature at the National University in Mexico City where he began writing poetry, and at Colombia University where he learned of Merton from Mark Van Doren, Merton's graduate studies advisor, and other friends of Merton. Returning home, Cardenal joined a plot against Somoza. Many friends of Cardenal were jailed, killed, exiled, or disappeared when the plot failed.

After a woman whom Cardenal loved married a Somoza protégé, Cardenal went to Gethsemani, where he came to know Merton in his role as novice master. Cardenal remained at Gethsemani two years. After Cardenal left Gethsemani, he wrote Merton but added that he did not want Merton to feel obliged to respond. "But I count on your prayers, as I always keep you in my own humble ones. I also keep the novices in my prayers too."[4]

Merton responded with compassion. Merton wrote that it was inevitable that Cardenal would experience feelings of being let down.

> You came here under ideal conditions, and everything was of a nature to make you happy and give you peace. You had given yourself completely to God without afterthought and without return, and He on His part had brought you to a place where the life was unexpectedly easy and pleasant and where everything went along quite smoothly for you. Hence in reality the first real Cross

2. Bochen, Review of *From the Monastery to the World*; in this article, Bochen discusses Cardenal's account of his time at Gethsemani. Cardenal reflected on his Gethsemani years in Wilkes, *Merton, by Those Who Knew Him Best.*

3. Gomes, "Pope Lifts Suspension"; Lopez, "Ernesto Cardenal, Nicaraguan Priest, Poet and Revolutionary, Dies at 95."

4. Letter 2, Cardenal to Merton, August 9, 1959, in Merton, *From the Monastery to the World*, 15.

you met with, in your response to God's call, was the necessity to *leave* this monastery, under obedience, after having been told that it was not God's will for you to stay here.

You must not regard this as the end of your vocation, or as a break in the progress of your soul toward God. On the contrary, it is an entirely necessary step and is part of the vital evolution of your vocation. It is a step in your spiritual maturity . . . For these last two years, Gethsemani was ideal for you, and you must regard it as a great grace that God brought you here. It is something that has changed the whole direction of your life. But at the same time if you had remained here, the general spirit of unrest in the community and the growing fear of falsity which have disturbed so many of our best vocations . . . would have reached you too.[5]

Merton did not explain "the general spirit of unrest in the community" to Cardenal. However, in his journal, Merton articulated his concern about the growing commercialization of life at the monastery.

Fr. Lawrence [Cardenal] left this morning. The last of those in whom I had originally placed hopes for a South American foundation and perhaps the best—a good poet, a good artist and one of the few genuine contemplatives in the place. But the life was giving him headaches and ulcers.

And again I am faced with the problem that this so-called contemplative monastery *ruins* real contemplatives, or makes life unbearable for them. Or can I say it is a "problem" when it has ceased to perplex me? Causes have effects. I am not absolutely sure I can point out the exact causes but in general: the place being a machine, an institution, in which personal values hardly count, in which what matters is the prosperity and reputation of the community and everything else comes after that.[6]

Journaling on December 5, 1959, Merton mentioned receiving a conscience letter from Cardenal.[7] This proved problematic for Abbot James Fox, who told Merton "blandly" that he (Fox) "would not give it to me. Instead he would return it to Mexico." Merton reflected ruefully, "This is a terrible thing. The whole attitude towards religion—a concept which is completely bound up with an unconscious, ingrained social prejudice . . . in favor of all that is firmly

5. Letter 3, Merton to Cardenal, August 17, 1959, in Merton, *From the Monastery to the World*, 15–16, Merton's emphasis.

6. Merton, *Search for Solitude*, 312, entry for July 30, 1959, Merton's emphasis.

7. Before Vatican II, writing conscience letters provided a window to the outside world.

established, the entrenched privilege of money, the unchangeable holiness of power." This reality enforced Merton's desire to move to Grand Chartreuse, a contemplative community in France. Merton mused,

> At times I feel fear that all the life is going to be inexorably squeezed out of me by this pious system, which, of course, I *must* obey, to which I *must* conform since I have vows. I really am beginning to understand the psalms, about the temptation to despair that beset the poor and the oppressed. To see what is evidently wrong or less good, triumph without difficulty while ideals of truth are crushed. There is no greater pain. Of course, it can always be said, "What is wrong with the setup, after all?" And if you look at it from a certain perspective—that of my abbot—you see no wrong in it at all. Nothing but good. I have rarely met anyone so completely comfortable in his acceptance of his own chosen delusions about life. Outside in the world—"power, pleasure, and popularity." In the monastery—the "cross." —They laugh—we suffer. And because we suffer, we are close to Jesus. But they don't laugh. They suffer and have more anguish than we do, even in their pleasures. We—vegetate and dream and sell cheese and get involved in petty projects. . . . In the cheese building they are all shouting about orders coming in.[8]

Cardenal first went to Mexico, where he visited Our Lady of the Resurrection, an experimental community led by Gregory Lemercier near Cuernavaca, Mexico. He also studied in Colombia, after which he returned to Nicaragua where a dream that had developed was realized. From 1965 to 1977, he was part of a community on Lake Nicaragua's Solentiname Islands, where he contributed to the growth of liberation theology.[9] From 1977 until 1987 he served in the Sandinista government as minister of culture.

At the time, intellectual ferment within the Catholic Church, and especially the spread of liberation theology throughout Latin America, led some Catholic leaders to oppose political engagement by clergy. Cardenal likely spoke for many contemporaries when he said, "No ecclesiastical document will stop us from doing what the Gospel tells us to do."[10]

Over time, Cardenal grew increasingly critical of Ortega's authoritarian style, Cardenal resigned from government. In a 2015 interview,

---

8. Merton, *Search for Solitude*, 351, entry for December 5, 1959, Merton's emphasis.

9. Examples of Ernesto Cardenal's writings include *Santidad en la Revolucion* (Buenos Aires, 1971), cited by Dussel, "Theology of Liberation and Marxism," 92; for an excerpt from *The Gospel of Solentiname*, see Cadorette et al., *Liberation Theology*, 230–35; also Galeano, *Memory of Fire*, 236; "Nicaragua: The Challenge of Revolution," 265–70.

10. Cited in Brown, "Significance of Puebla," 331.

he conceded that, though the Marxist revolution had failed, he remained committed to its ideals.

> I am a revolutionary [which] means that I want to change the world. . . . The Bible is full of revolutions. The prophets are people with a message of revolution. Jesus of Nazareth takes the revolutionary message of the prophets. And we also will continue trying to change the world and make revolution. Those revolutions failed, but others will come.[11]

Recalling Merton's interest in Latin America beginning with his trip to Cuba in 1940, we can understand why Merton welcomed Cardenal's presence at Gethsemani. During the 1950s, Merton had entertained the idea of establishing a foundation in Ecuador. As well, Merton read books and poetry by South American authors. Between 1957 and 1959, some of the novices, in addition to Cardenal, spoke Spanish. As novice master, Merton was spiritual director for Cardenal, who provided Merton addresses of Latin American poets and poetry magazines. Cardenal translated some of Merton's poetry into Spanish.

Despite leaving Gethsemani, Cardenal sustained and deepened his friendship with Merton. Writing to Cardenal on November 17, 1962, Merton referred to having had a great deal of trouble with censors. He indicated that he had resorted to being published in England whenever he wrote something at risk of reprobation in the Order, anything more than statements like "It is nice to pray. Good morning Father, have some holy waters. We never eat hot dogs on Friday."[12]

Merton considered transferring to a monastery in Mexico. This proved impossible in part because the Benedictine order required monks to remain at one monastery and prohibited "particular friendships." Uneasy about the Merton-Cardenal relationship, Fox initially forbade communication but later approved their corresponding. For a period of fifteen months, more than a year after Merton was barred from leaving Gethsemani for a new foundation in Latin America, Merton did not write Cardenal. It is unclear if Merton received any letters from Cardenal, who was aware of the situation. Merton resolved "to take no further positive steps as long as I live, to leave the Order."[13]

---

11. Lopez, "Ernesto Cardenal, Nicaraguan Priest, Poet and Revolutionary." Ortega was elected president of Nicaragua and has served from 1985 to 1990, and since 2007.

12. Letter 36, Merton to Cardenal, November 17, 1962, in Merton, *From the Monastery to the World*, 118.

13. Merton to Fox, December 17, 1959, in Merton, *Witness to Freedom*, 214.

Biographer Michael Mott wrote that Merton told Abbot Fox that Cardenal needed Merton's advice on spiritual matters, to which Fox replied [according to Merton] that he [Merton] was far too busy to give advice and at such distance; others, nearer at hand, could advise him [Cardinal].[14]

In her review of the Merton-Cardenal correspondence, Christine Bochen highlighted three themes: vocation in the religious sense and in the broader sense of a calling to writing as a life's work; speaking truth in times of crisis; and the recovery of unity. In this chapter, I focus on Merton's role as ally to Cardenal, a leading poet, contemplative, and liberation theologian at a time of renewal in the Catholic Church.

Learning Cardenal would receive Jesuit formation *gratis*, Merton wrote, "This is another evident sign of God's love for you, and with all peace and joy you should accept it, with no anxiety and care about where or how you will exercise this priesthood when the time comes."[15] As he awaited word whether he would be permitted to move from Gethsemani, Merton wrote,

> Prayers are the most important thing at the moment. And deep faith. The inertia of conventional religious life is like a deep sleep from which one only awakens from time to time, to realize how deeply he has been sleeping. Then he falls back into it. It is true that God works here also, but there are so many influences to deaden and falsify the interior life. A kind of perpetual danger of sclerosis. The psalms become more and more of a comfort, more and more full of meaning when one realizes that they do *not* apply to the conventional situations, but to another kind of situation altogether. The psalms are for poor men, or solitary men, or men who suffer: not for liturgical enthusiasts in a comfortable, well-heated choir.[16]

On December 24, 1961, Merton reported that his (Merton's) concept of the church and faith in the church were being tested, purified, and radically challenged. "I am deeply concerned about peace and am united in working with other Christians for protest against nuclear war."[17]

On March 4, 1962, Cardenal acknowledged receipt of Merton's letter as well as copies of *New Seeds of Contemplation* and *Disputed Questions*. For

14. Mott, *Seven Mountains of Thomas Merton*, 339–40

15. Letter 6, Merton to Cardenal, September 12, 1959, in Merton, *From the Monastery to the World*, 27.

16. Letter 10, Merton to Cardenal, November 18, 1959, in Merton, *From the Monastery to the World*, 50, Merton's emphasis.

17. Letter 23, Merton to Cardenal, December 24, 1961, in Merton, *From the Monastery to the World*, 84.

Cardenal, these books addressed issues such as peace and social action that resonated with developments in Latin America. Cardenal highlighted Merton's "Letter to Pablo Antonio Cuadra Concerning Giants."[18]

A cousin of Cardenal, Cuadra (1912–2002) was a prominent Nicaraguan poet. He edited a literary journal, *El Pez y la Serpiente* (The Fish and the Serpent) and coedited *La Prensa* (The Press). *The Courage for Truth* included some of Merton's letters to him.[19] Merton's translations of Cuadra's poems and book, *The Jaguar and the Moon*, were also published.[20]

In his letter to Cuadra, which circulated widely in the Hispanic world, Merton argued that "the greatest sin of the European-Russian-American complex that we call 'the West' is not only greed and cruelty, not only moral dishonesty and infidelity to truth, but above all in an *unmitigated arrogance toward the rest of the human race*." Merton deemed the West's assault on the stranger, notably indigenous populations, as well as an absence of Christian humanism, as an affront to the mystery of the incarnation. For Merton, this was a disloyalty to the Word made Flesh, God in man, because "God is in *all men* and all men are to be seen and treated as Christ."[21]

Between 1962 and 1965, the Merton-Cardenal exchange overlapped with meetings of the Second Ecumenical Council of the Vatican, commonly known as Vatican II. In an undated letter written in 1963, Merton wrote that he thought the meetings were "going well. . . . The collegiality of bishops is one of the most important things done by the Church in the last five hundred years . . . . If lay deacons (even married) are allowed, this can have tremendous significance, especially in Latin America."[22]

Merton also affirmed enthusiastically Cardenal's work with Indians: "I think this is really a very important project, and coming just at the right time it can have a decisive effect, both spiritual and cultural, throughout Latin America."[23]

Merton encouraged Cardenal to reach out to Nicaragua's indigenous population. This reflected Merton's conviction that one can learn from the

18. Letter 24, Cardenal to Merton, March 4, 1962, in Merton, *From the Monastery to the World*, and 27–30 and 267–75 for Merton's "Letter to Pablo Antonio Cuadra."

19. Merton, *Courage for Truth*, 178–95.

20. Merton's translations of Cuadra's poems and book, *The Jaguar and the Moon* (1974); biographical background, *From the Monastery to the World*, 284–85.

21. Merton, *From the Monastery to the World*, 267–68, Merton's emphasis.

22. Letter 48, Merton to Cardenal, no date, in Merton, *From the Monastery to the World*, 149.

23. Letter 48, Merton to Cardenal, no date, in Merton, *From the Monastery to the World*, 149. For Merton's interest in Native Americans, see my "Ishi: Messenger of Hope," chapter 4 in this book.

traditions of First Peoples of the Americas, including the Inca and Maya cultures overwhelmed during the Spanish conquest. Writing in *Mystics and Zen Masters*, Merton observed, "Our task now is to learn that if we can voyage to the ends of the earth and there find ourselves in the aborigine who most differs from ourselves, we will have made a fruitful pilgrimage."[24]

On November 13, 1963, Cardenal responded, "Every day I become more interested in Indian-related things and am learning more from them. . . . I owe you for my ability to begin to understand and love the Indians, and most of all for being able to see in them the religious and spiritual values that I did not see."[25]

On July 12, 1964, Merton reiterated his appreciation of Cardenal's reaching out to Indians. "It is . . . important to listen to the silence of the Indians and to admit to hearing all that has not been said for five hundred years. The salvation of our lives depends on it."[26] Merton also affirmed Cardenal's ordination and priestly vocation.

From 1965 until 1968, Merton lived in a hermitage on the Abbey of Gethsemani grounds. This paralleled Cardenal's time at Solentiname, a place of retreat that facilitated contemplation and growth. In 1967, James Fox retired and Flavian Burns was elected abbot at Gethsemani. This opened a possibility for Merton to travel outside of Gethsemani, perhaps relocating to a new hermit colony in California, or elsewhere. As well, it reflected the spirit of Vatican II, sometimes characterized as *aggiornamento*, Latin for "bringing up to date," a phrase used by Pope John XXIII in a speech he gave on January 25, 1959 to indicate his desire to open the Roman Catholic Church for dialogue with the wider world.

In one of his last letters to Cardenal, Merton expressed his hope to visit Solentiname when he returned home from the monastic conference in Thailand to which he had been invited, and given permission to attend. Merton indicated this would not be a permanent move. He feared that he would be "something of a tourist attraction. . . . If I were to leave here, I would want to disappear completely and go where I was not known at all, and cease to have any kind of public existence whatever."[27]

24. See "From Pilgrimage to Crusade" in Merton, *Mystics and Zen Masters*, 112.

25. Letter 49, Cardenal to Merton, November 13, 1963, in Merton, *From the Monastery to the World*, 151.

26. Letter 56, Merton to Cardenal, July 12, 1964, in Merton, *From the Monastery to the World*, 168.

27. Letter 89, Merton to Cardenal, March 15, 1968, in Merton, *From the Monastery to the World*, 239.

In this brief survey of some of the Merton-Cardenal correspondence, several themes appear. One is Merton's deep appreciation of fellow poets. In one essay, Merton wrote,

> There is a mental ecology . . . a living balance of spirits in this corner of the woods. There is room here for many other songs besides those of birds. Of Vallejo, for instance. Or Rilke, or René Char, Montale, Zukofsky, Ungaretti, Edwin Muir, Quasimodo, or some Greeks. Or the dry, disconcerting voice of Nicanor Parra, the poet of the sneeze. Here is also Chuang Tzu whose climate is perhaps most the climate of this silent corner of woods. A climate in which there is no need for explanations. Here is the reassuring companionship of many silent Tzu's and Fu's; Kung Tzu, Lao Tzu, Meng Tzu, Tu Fu. And Jui Neng. And Chao-Chu. And the drawings of Sengai. And a big graceful scroll from Suzuki. Here also is a Syrian hermit called Philoxenus. An Algerian cenobite called Camus. Here is heard the clanging prose of Tertullian, with the dry catarrh of Sartre. Here the voluble dissonances of Auden, with the golden sounds of John of Salisbury. Here is the deep vegetation of that more ancient forest in which the angry birds, Isaias and Jeremias, sing. Here should be, and are, feminine voices from Angela of Foligno to Flannery O'Connor, Theresa of Avila, Juliana of Norwich, and, more personally . . . Raissa Maritain. It is good to choose the voices that will be heard in these woods, but they also choose themselves, and send themselves here to be present in this silence.[28]

Merton embraced others. Merton pioneered monastic interfaith dialogue. Merton valued dialogue, difference, and diversity. He thus provided a model for us some sixty years later at a time when many see others—the foreigner, the stranger, one whose life style differs from the mainstream, or the outsider—in less positive a manner. To paraphrase words of the musical *South Pacific*, many are being led and taught very deliberately to hate. By contrast, Merton wrote,

> [One] who has attained final integration is no longer limited by the culture in which he has grown up. "He has embraced *all of life*. . . ." He accepts not only his own community, his own society, his own culture, but all mankind. He does not remain bound to one limited set of values in such a way that he opposes them aggressively or defensively to others. He is fully "Catholic" in the best sense of the word . . . and is a peacemaker, and that

28. Merton, "Day of a Stranger," 432–33.

is why there is such a desperate need for our leaders to become such men of insight.[29]

Through the ages, many Christians have failed to live out the love ethic manifest in God's sacrificial act in Jesus' crucifixion. This is so for many reasons among which history, cultural blindness, nationalism, ideology, and failure to recognize our common humanity. In this concluding chapter exploring his legacy, Thomas Merton in dialogue with Ernesto Cardenal called all humanity to practice dialogue and embrace and to reject confrontation, hateful speech, or violence.

This calling motivated me in part to write this book. Merton and Cardenal offer a positive way forward amidst the violence and some of the rhetoric manifest in 2020. At a very personal level, I have drawn inspiration from Merton for much of my life, beginning with my university years when I began to read articles and books by him. In 1986, I participated in a "friendship visit" to Nicaragua organized by the Baptist Peace Fellowship of North America.[30] Preparing to travel, I read in English some of Cardenal's poetry. I hoped our delegation might meet Cardenal. This did not materialize. The trip did enable me to travel to El Salvador where I met family members of refugees who had been sponsored in Canada by the congregation in Hamilton, Ontario of which I was then a member, MacNeill Baptist Church.

As I prepared to depart, my wife asked if I would be in danger. I confessed that both countries were conflict zones. I explained further that members of the congregations hosting us worked with the poor and daily risked being confused with so-called guerilla groups that did pose a military threat to the governments. Nonetheless, I believed it unlikely that the governments of either country, let alone of the United States or Canada, would countenance an attack on citizens on a peace delegation.

In both countries, I heard sounds of gunfire. On one occasion, I observed soldiers "recruiting" young men from the village into active military service. I recalled a poster I saw in the home of my hosts: "Todo ninos es Jesus con nosotros." Every child is Jesus with us.

In 1992, I returned to these communities after I attended an international peace conference in Nicaragua. President Daniel Ortega was a speaker. On a third occasion, in 1996, I traveled to both countries to

29. Merton, *Contemplation in a World of Action*, 225–26, Merton's emphasis; also the 1998 edition, 207.

30. Dekar, "Baptist Friendship Tour to Nicaragua," 6. See my "Peacemaking in Central America" and "Compassion: Central America's Only Hope."

research the possible relevance of Dr. King's legacy for nonviolent justice seekers in Latin America.[31]

Such engagement enabled me to affirm the importance of international allies in a conflict region. In word and deed, we established solidarity with Nicaraguans seeking to promote a better, more peaceful world through nonviolent means. In words of the World Social Forum, we believed that "another world is possible."[32]

Through their correspondence, Merton and Cardenal embraced such a vision. Continuing until his untimely death, such letters enabled Merton to be an ally and friend to Cardenal in their mutual search to build a society compatible with biblical justice, compassion, love, and truth.

31. The outcome was my article, "Martin Luther King Jr. and Nonviolent Justice Seekers in Latin America and the Caribbean," published in *Nonviolence for the Third Millennium*, edited by the late G. Simon Harak, 137–54.

32. The World Social Forum is an annual meeting of civil society organizations in the Global South, promoting alternatives to economic priorities of the superpowers at the World Economic Forum's Annual Meeting in Davos, Switzerland. In 2006, I attended the sixth in Venezuela, and, the next year, a parallel gathering in North America. Such advocacy efforts by social movements seeking international solidarity resonate with the concerns discussed by Merton and Cardenal in their correspondence.

Section Five: **Reviews**

Phillip M. Thompson, *Returning to Reality: Thomas Merton's Wisdom for a Technological World* (Eugene, OR: Cascade, 2012).

Technology, a preoccupation in some of Merton's writings, is evident in my review entitled "Community or Collectivity?" To explore "Merton's wisdom for a technology world," Phillip M. Thompson frames his study through a polarity, collectivity versus community. The former paradigm prioritizes material progress and prosperity; promotes science; is obsessed with productivity; favors reason over spirituality; and generates mindless technologies that dull human imagination and manipulate people. The latter "spiritual vision" prioritizes moral growth and the dignity of every person; promotes a humanizing conception of work; supports spiritual and rational forms of knowledge; produces technologies that sharpen the intellect; and integrates body, mind, and soul.

Through writing, mentoring, and visits by friends, Merton became a spiritual director for Abbey of Gethsemani monks and wider communities of resistance. Especially in the last ten years of his life, Merton worried about the impact of technology in three areas that Thompson explores at length: "avoiding the nuclear apocalypse"; "reforming the information age"; and "choosing to be human or transhuman."

Thompson believes Merton remains pertinent for a "superficial and distracted consumers of instant messages and images" (ix). Stressing that Merton did not eschew technology, Thompson highlights Merton's call for balance and prescience regarding "The distorted desire for cloning and prolonging life are examples of a materialism that radically manipulates creation" (71).

I recall reading Merton in the early 1960s when I studied at the University of California, Berkeley. I resonated with Merton's critique of a society obsessed with "the technological furies of size, volume, quantity, speed, number, price, power and acceleration" (*Raids on the Unspeakable*, 70). I joined protests and wore badges with slogans such as "you can't hug a child with nuclear arms," "the meek are getting ready," "we cannot change unless we survive but we will not survive unless we change," and "EVERYONE MAKES A DIFFERENCE." On one of my favorites, a whale wears a button with the words, "save the humans."

Merton's wisdom paralleled insights of another Berkeley contemporary, Mario Savio of the Free Speech Movement. At a December 3, 1964 rally, the latter affirmed, "There is a time when the operation of the machine becomes so odious, makes you so sick at heart, that you can't take part; you can't even passively take part, and you've got to put your bodies upon the gears and upon the wheels, upon the levers, upon all the apparatus and you've got to indicate to the people who run it, to the people who own it, that unless you're free, the machine will be prevented from working at all!"

Consider insights of cartoonists. For example, *The Hamilton Spectator* has carried *Blondie* since the 1930s. On January 15, 2013, Dagwood's boss, Julius Caesar Dithers, asks his wife Cora, "What's all this Facebook nonsense with people posting pics of their feet?" She replies, "Oh, it's to show they're lounging on vacation." In the second frame, she says, "See? They snap foot photos on lazy, relaxing backgrounds like beaches or pools . . . or in some cases their desks." Frame three shows Dagwood Bumstead, smartphone in his hand, photographing his feet on his workplace desk.

The *Between Friends* comic strip in *The Hamilton Spectator* for January 16, 2013 began with a homemaker struggling to find a source of intellectual fulfilment. She taps on her computer. She thinks, "I am bored with Facebook minutiae." The second frame shows her posting her input. The third frame shows her friends' responses: "like like like like like like like . . . ." In the final frame, Kimberly observes, "There's something seriously wrong with our culture."

I suspect Thompson and Merton would concur. Combining analysis and jeremiad, Thompson's book deserves wide readership. He might celebrate the action of a friend whose emails announce, "Normally I keep Monday as a 'hermitage' day, and as part of this I am offline from Sunday evening until Tuesday morning." I have followed suit, refusing to become software.

Christoffer H. Grundmann, ed. *Interreligious Dialogue: An Anthology of Voices Bridging Cultural and Religious Divides* (Winona, MN: Anselm Academic, 2015).

This collection of fourteen essays published over the past ten years includes five non-Christian authors: Jonathan Sacks (Jewish); Swami Tyagananda and K. L. Seshagiri Rao (Hindu); Seyyed Hussein Nasr (Muslim); and Havanpola Ratanasara (Buddhist). The other contributions are by two Christian pioneers of interfaith dialogue.

In one piece, Catholic theologian Paul R. Knitter cites Thomas Berry, one of the most forceful of "earth-prophets." In 1983, Berry anticipated "concern for the wellbeing of the planet is the one concern that hopefully will bring the nations [and religions] of the world into an inter-nation [and interreligious] community" (37).

In another, Thomas Merton opens "Apologies to an Unbeliever," which first appeared in *Faith and Violence* (1968), "This is not going to be an easy tune to sing" (85). Merton expresses secretly to be grateful for refusing to accept so much of the arrogant dictation that they ("believers") have tried to foist on you (86). He goes on to describe his particular vocation in the world in terms that, when I first read it decades earlier, I quoted it in a paper prepared for my ordination committee.

In his essay "Inter-religious Living in an Age of Globalization," Methodist Martin Forward, founder of the Centre for the Study of Jewish-Christian Relations at Cambridge, England, notes insights of Canadian historian and theologian of religion Wilfred Cantwell Smith. In myriad writings, Smith highlighted pre-requisites of interreligious dialogue: assurance of safety; language study; community-building; immersing oneself in the faith of another who can affirm "you know me."

I appreciated the elegant layout of the book and helpful introductions to each essay by the editor. Grundmann, Professor of Religion and Healing Arts at Valparaiso University, concludes with three helpful tips on "'How to Get Moving?': Think Outside the Box of Conventional Wisdom; Dare to Trust the Religious Other; and Stay Authentic." He also provided a helpful appendix with Internet Resources.

I found reading, or rereading, the essays helpful. I especially appreciated the authors' focus on practical, non-doctrinal issues. The only piece by practitioners working principally outside the United States or Britain is "Youth in Interfaith Dialogue: Intercultural Understanding and its Implications on Education in the Philippines," by Jayeel S. Cornelio and Timothy Andrew E. Salera. The voices of women are absent. Unfamiliar with the publisher, I went to its website and found a refreshing list of books.

Charles L. Cohen, Paul F. Knitter, and Ulrich Rosenhagen, eds., *The Future of Interreligious Dialogue: A Multireligious Conversation on Nostra Aetate* (Maryknoll, NY: Orbis, 2017).

Shortly after his election in 1958, Pope John XXIII interrupted a liturgy when one of the celebrants used the word "perfidious" to describe Jews. The pope had the prayer repeated without the offending word. He later greeted a Jewish delegation, "I am Joseph, your brother." This marked the start of a new relationship between Jews and Catholics and served as prequel to Vatican II, arguably one of the most transformative religious events of the last century. *Nostra Aetate*, the declaration on the relation of the Roman Catholic Church to non-Christian religions, was one of the council's most fruitful outcomes. This book arose from a conference fifty years after that document's release.

Seventeen essays provide Christian, Jewish, Muslim, Buddhist, and Hindu perspectives. Each paper is confessional, scholarly, and challenging. Key issues include nonsupersessionist Christology and the doctrine of creation. Seven authors are women. Notably absent are aboriginal authors or those of smaller religions such as the Druze or Jains. Congregations, classes, or dialogue groups may invite guests to facilitate discussion of a chapter by faith community members.

For a short review, I highlight paths for future dialogue presented by John J. Thatamanil of Union Theological Seminary in New York City. What might a new *Nostra Aetate* include? The church would reaffirm that it rejects nothing "that is true and holy in [other] religions." As the Apostle Paul and the church with him learned from Greek philosophers to speak of God as the one in whom "we live and move and have our being" (Acts 17:28), the church would gratefully acknowledge that it has been and continues to be enriched by the gifts of wisdom and the Spirit that God has granted in every age to God's children who are not church members. The church would confess in humility that it does not know all there is to know about the Word become flesh. The church would recognize the profound depth of the riches of other faith communities. Aware of the importance of debate, the church would welcome to dialogue in openness, respect, and friendship. Calling the world to care for imperiled Earth, the church would seek to work with indigenous traditions to acknowledge, preserve, promote, and receive the wisdom of First Nations peoples. I have benefitted from such dialogue prompted by a document of parallel magnitude, Francis's encyclical letter *Laudato Si* on care for our common home.

Stan Chu Ilo, *A Poor and Merciful Church: The Illuminative Ecclesiology of Pope Francis* (Maryknoll, NY: Orbis, 2018).

This book highlights Catholicism as church of the poor and of mercy under Pope Francis. Born in Argentina in 1936, Jorge Mario Bergoglio is the first pope to have come from the Americas. During these early years of his pontificate, Francis has highlighted his understanding of the church as bruised, hurting, dirty, unconcerned with being at the center of abuse charges, and caught in a web of obsessions and procedures.

Nigerian by birth, Stan Chu Ilo is research professor and coordinator of the African Catholicism Project at DePaul University. In this, his fifth book, he highlights Pope Francis's "culture of encounter." Ilo considers this a significant shift from Rome to the margins. Francis is thus a liberation theologian in a tradition extending from Las Casas in the sixteenth century through Paulo Freire, Gustavo Gutiérrez, and Óscar Romero, along with twentieth-century Protestants Dietrich Bonhoeffer, Martin Luther King Jr., and Rosemary Ruether.

Addressing the questions, "Why another book on Pope Francis?" and "Who is the church?" Ilo argues that many people live in fidelity to Jesus. In particular, Francis has shown the face of the Holy in Jesus through living as an exemplar of poverty and mercy. Ilo illustrates the pope's "theology from below" by citing the example of "a famous light-bearer," Mother Teresa of Calcutta. Two years after she visited Australia, she received a letter from an Aboriginal Australian whom she had met. He wanted her to know that "the light you lit in my life continues to shine still." Ilo uses this story to show how Pope Francis has taught Catholics and indeed all people to live the commandment of Jesus to be salt and light of the world (30).

After an introduction, chapter 2 explores the Biblical, historical, and theological foundations of the theme. Ilo recalls an event during the "Holy Year of Mercy" (December 8, 2015–November 20, 2016). The pope wrote *Evangelii Gaudium* in which he appealed, "I want a church which is poor and for the poor" (85). This, his first "poor-teaching" invited all Christians to return to the true evangelical path that has guided authentic living through the centuries.

Looking beyond the papacy of Francis, Ilo offers a praxis of illuminative ecclesiology, a road map that all can follow. *A Poor and Merciful Church World* presents a vulnerable missiology for a deeply hurting world. I commend this book for group discussion. I have participated in one. We read and discussed *Laudato Sí*, Praise Be To You, Pope Francis's 2015 encyclical letter on the environment. Participants—all Protestants—welcomed of Francis's leadership on so pressing an issue. Writing this review on October 4, the feast day of Saint Francis, I welcome Ilo's passionate call to faithful living.

Hugh Turley and David Martin, *The Martyrdom of Thomas Merton: An Investigation* (Hyattsville, MD: McCabe, 2018).

Hugh Turley, volunteer columnist for the *Hyattsville Life and Times*, and David Martin, who works for the Bureau of Labor Statistics, argue that Thomas Merton did not die by accidental electrocution. Rather, Merton was murdered on orders from the Central Intelligence Agency of the United States. This review summarizes and critiques their case.

Turley and Martin begin by presenting the generally-accepted-account of Merton's death. In December 1968 at a monastic gathering near Bangkok, Thailand, Merton gave a talk, "Marxism and Monastic Perspectives." After lunch, he retired to his room. Sometime later, a participant heard what he thought were a cry and the sound of something falling. Somewhat later again, Merton was found on his back with a fan lying across his body. A local doctor concluded that Merton died of cardiac failure from electrical shock. Without reason to suspect criminal cause, authorities deemed Merton's death was from a "natural cause" (63) and allowed the body to be returned to the United States. No autopsy was performed.

In his biography, Michael Mott wrote that the evidence overwhelmingly pointed to accidental electrocution as the cause of Merton's death. Mott offered a "most likely reconstruction of events" according to which, after a shower, Merton may have slipped on a faulty fan that gave Merton a shock sufficient in itself to kill him as he cried out, or which induced a massive heart attack. Mott acknowledged that there were a number of unanswered questions and that it was a matter of "real regret" that Merton's death was investigated in a bungled and amateurish fashion and that there was no autopsy. Mott discounted suicide or murder.

Turley and Martin build an alternative hypothesis regarding Merton's death from eyewitness accounts, interviews, "curiosities" (19), and letters from conference participant Celestine Say, a Benedictine monk from the Philippines, to Abbot Flavian Burns and to John Howard Griffin. Discounting Mott's version, Turley and Martin write that the first accounts of Merton's death did not mention that Merton had taken a shower.

The official reports from the Thai authorities said nothing about a bath or a shower. The popular story that water was involved in Merton's electrocution was likely invented because it is common knowledge that touching an electric appliance while in a bath or shower can be fatal. On the other hand, a fatal electrocution from simply touching a household appliance is virtually unheard of. The story that Merton was electrocuted from touching a fan while wet from a shower is particularly vile and insidious because it manages to blame a likely assassination victim of killing himself through his own carelessness (109).

In Part 3, entitled "the enemies of the truth," Turley and Martin accuse Mott and other biographers as well as Merton's monastic colleagues for selling Merton short. They contend that the US government deemed Merton sufficiently dangerous that they plotted and carried out Merton's death to silence his voice against war and for social justice. They conclude,

> Contrary to the common view, there is really no mystery about how Merton died. The best evidence indicates beyond any serious doubt that Merton was murdered. It's a simple fact that the average person is far more likely to be murdered than to be killed by an electric fan, and Merton was no average person. The story that a fan killed Merton is so preposterous that a series of fantastic stories have had to be invented to make it believable . . . .Who did it and why? . . . . The CIA had the motive and the means. (267)

In terms of motive, the authors cite a letter from Matthew Kelty, a monastic colleague of Merton, to the effect that Merton had been a problem to many at the abbey (216). A wider motivation for Merton's executioners was that they saw Merton as a threat. Merton "was completely independent and thoroughly incorruptible and . . . was reaching a large and influential audience. One might well imagine how much greater influence he might have had if he had lived out a natural life. The only way to shut him up was to kill him" (268).

As for means, the authors cite a CIA manual as follows: "For secret assassination . . . the contrived accident is the most effective technique" (202). The authors write that the CIA had, in 1958, illegally opened and resealed a letter from Merton to Russian writer Boris Pasternak. The CIA carried Merton on a watch list to intercept his mail to the Soviet Union. "CIA is particularly adept at killing people and . . . use a wide assortment of methods" (206–7). The authors do not, however, indicate which method the CIA allegedly used to take Merton out.

Turley and Martin provide fresh documentation regarding Merton's death. They also set Merton's death in the social and political climate in the United States in the 1960s. Sociologist Todd Gitlin characterized the decade as "Years of hope, days of rage." In *JFK and the Unspeakable: Why*

He Died and Why It Matters, James W. Douglass similarly sets the death of President Kennedy in a wider social context. In *The Assassination of Robert F. Kennedy: Crime, Conspiracy and Cover-Up; a New Investigation*, Tim Tate and Brad Johnson explore various theories about the murder of Robert Kennedy during his 1968 campaign for the Democratic Party presidential nomination. Others have investigated the deaths of Malcolm X, Dr. Martin Luther King Jr., and Vincent Foster.

For me, the authors fail to satisfy a criterion operating when I have served on juries, namely, to establish beyond reasonable doubt that Merton was murdered. Barring access to CIA documents, I am not clear what new evidence may strengthen the authors' case.

More disconcerting, the authors claim that Brother Patrick Hart and Abbot Flavian Burns played a crucial role in a cover-up. They thereby charge members of Merton's community with complicity in his death. Over the years, I have done retreats at the Abbey of Gethsemani and attended many Merton-related conferences. I have talked with many of Merton's brothers, including Hart, and concluded that the generally accepted account of Merton's death by accidental electrocution is plausible.

Another question concerns a key word in the title. Why "martyrdom"? The word means witness. During the first, second, and third centuries of the modern era, and more recently, martyrs have refused to abandon faith in the face of persecution. Saint Óscar Romero warrants the title. So do Maryknoll Sisters Ita Ford and Maura Clarke, along with Ursuline Sister Dorothy Kazel and lay missioner Jean Donovan. All were martyred during the 1980s in El Salvador.

By contrast, the death of the most important Roman Catholic spiritual writer of his day was tragic. But the authors of the book under review have not convinced me that Merton was a martyr.

The authors rightly argue that Merton's purported murderer(s) did not achieve their supposed end, namely, to silence Merton. Successive generations of readers around the world have found wisdom for living from reading Merton. The authors of the book under review do raise important questions that should engender more-than-usual comment and further research.

Susan McCaslin and J. S Porter, *Superabundantly Alive: Thomas Merton's Dance with the Feminine* (Kelona: Wood Lake, 2018), review in *Hamilton Arts and Letters*, December 2018.

Thomas Merton (1915–68) was an influential post-Second World War figure for many Catholics and non-Catholics alike. His writings—for example, his essay "The Root of War is Fear" and poetry like *Original Child Bomb: Points for Meditation to Be Scratched on the Walls of a Cave*—inspired both authors of this fresh revisiting of Merton's legacy.

A poet living in British Colombia, Susan McCaslin writes, "Merton . . . encourages people within and without traditional religions to plumb their own inner depths and engage with issues of social justice" (20). Hamiltonian J. S. Porter observes, "Thomas Merton has a surprising capacity to pop up in places you may not expect. He is still alive in our culture, a quiet presence in recited prayers at addiction meetings . . . [and] in words on love at weddings and even at funerals. His words encourage, challenge, scold, provoke, console, and humble" (29).

Merton is most frequently remembered for his autobiography, *The Seven Storey Mountain* (1948), and his writings in the 1960s on prayer, interfaith, and social issues. This book focuses on the person, especially one who struggled with gender relationships. I found especially moving Susan McCaslin's imagined exchanges of Merton with women in his life: his mother Ruth Jenkins: Catholic Saints like Thérèse de Lisieux; Margie, the nurse with whom Merton fell in love; writers like Julian of Norwich and Dorothy Day; the musician Joan Baez; and others.

During a speech in 2015 before the United States Congress, Pope Francis singled out Merton as one of four "great Americans" along with Dorothy Day, John F. Kennedy, and Martin Luther King Jr. The pope described Merton as "above all a man of prayer, a thinker who challenged the certitudes of his time and opened new horizons for souls and for the church. He was also a man of dialogue, a promoter of peace between peoples and religions." The monk's contribution to America's cultural reserves, the pope said, falls under our capacity to pursue dialogue.

Writing this review on December 10, 2018, fifty years to the day of his death, I am struck by how Thomas Merton still challenges readers to pursue dialogue on interreligious, gender, and other social issues. This book, a compilation of essays and poetry some of which have been published elsewhere, may inspire general readers who do not know Merton's writings to explore his ever-vital literary output. For Merton aficionados, this book captures afresh the prophetic spirit of one who, as Merton's friend Robert Lax wrote, was "superabundantly alive."

Concluding Reflections

AT THE START I asked, does Merton still matter? Absolutely! By his critique of technology, his teaching on contemplative prayer; his interfaith outreach, and his prophetic witness against racism, war, and degradation of nature. Merton still matters. An African-American correspondent of Merton, Robert Lawrence Williams called Merton a messenger of God who dreamed of a new world. Merton still calls people to act for the greater common good.

John Lennon of the Beatles is sometimes quoted as saying, "Everything will be okay in the end. If it's not okay, it's not the end." The world is not okay. However, humanity does not necessarily face an apocalyptic ending. What can an individual do to make a difference? I have found helpful several exercises that anyone can adapt for her or his daily meditation time, or in communal worship. Let me share two. One is to recall Gandhi's talisman. It goes as follows:

> I will give you a talisman. Whenever you are in doubt, or when the self becomes too much with you, apply the following test. Recall the face of the poorest and the weakest man [woman] whom you may have seen, and ask yourself, if the step you contemplate is going to be of any use to him [her]. Will he [she] gain anything by it? Will it restore him [her] to a control over his [her] own life and destiny? In other words, will it lead to *swaraj* [freedom] for the hungry and spiritually starving millions? Then you will find your doubts and your self melting away.[1]

I practice another exercise in Quaker worship. I learned the exercise from Thich Nhat Hahn. In meditation, I name each person present, thinking,

1. I carry a copy of "The Gandhi Talisman" in my diary.

May he/she be peaceful, happy, and light in body and in spirit. May he/she be free from injury. May he/she live in safety. May he/she be free from anger, disturbance, fear, worry, and anxiety." As you concentrate on another. . . . if she lives east of you, send your energy to the east. If she is sitting to your right, extend your energy to the right. Surround her with the energy of love. Even if she is not in need of your love, practice this way. Dwell in deep concentration. Because you know how to love yourself, you have the capacity to offer love to someone you like. Look deeply into her . . . body, feelings, perceptions, mental formations, and consciousness. This practice is quite easy.[2]

In *Speak Truth to Power: A Quaker Search for an Alternative to Violence*, written in 1955, friends of Merton, including A. J. Muste and Amiya Chakravarty, offered a challenge with which Merton would have resonated. The Quaker group affirmed that faith is relevant, that humanity has a higher destiny than self-destruction, and that a way to meet the forces of disintegration that threatened then, and now, is to do the following:

To release into society integrated men and women, whose lives are at one with God, with themselves and with their fellow men . . . [and a] sense of community, of mutuality, of responsible brotherhood for all men everywhere. Such a community is built on trust and confidence, which some will say is not possible now because the communist cannot be trusted. The politics of eternity does not require that we trust him. They require us to love him and to trust God. Our affirmation in this day is that of John Woolman in his: I have no cause to promote but the cause of pure universal love." We call for no calculated risk on behalf of national interest or preservation; rather for an uncalculated risk in living by the claims of the kingdom, on behalf of the whole family of man conceived as a divine-human society.[3]

Writing in 2020 amidst a global pandemic, racial violence in the United States, and threats to use nuclear weapons, I recall Merton's dis-ease with legislation. He saw passage of the Civil Rights Act of 1964 and Voting Rights Act of 1965 as necessary but insufficient. Why? He thought the laws failed to address structures that sustain systemic evil. Reflecting on the situation in the United States and the world in the 1960s, Merton wrote,

The only way out of this fantastic impasse is for everyone to face and accept the difficulties and sacrifices involved, in all their

2. Nhat Hahn, *Essential Writings*, 104.
3. AFSC, *Speak Truth to Power*, 68–69.

seriousness, in all their inexorable demands. This is what our society, based on a philosophy of every man for himself and on the rejection of altruism and sacrifice (except in their most schematic and imaginary forms) is not able to do. Yet it is something which it must learn to do. It cannot begin to learn unless it knows the need to learn. These "Letters" attempt to demonstrate the urgency of the situation.[4]

Nearly sixty years later, Merton's words of caution remain prophetic. Recognizing the urgency of life on earth in 2020, I believe with Merton that "the God of peace is never glorified by violence."[5] I offer this book in the hope it will inspire people, in words often attributed to Gandhi, to be the change you wish to see in the world. Do justice. Be compassionate. Walk humbly with God. Live the truth. Embrace divinity in yourself, and in others.

Merton spoke words in Thailand to Buddhist and Christian monks that, unexpectedly and tragically, summarized what he thought essential in the monastic life.

[It] is not embedded in buildings, is not embedded in clothing, is not necessarily embedded even in a rule. It is somewhere along the line of something deeper than a rule. It is concerned with this business of total inner transformation. All other things serve that end. I am just saying, in other words, what Cassian said in the first lecture on *puritas cordis,* purity of heart, that every monastic observance tends toward that.[6]

In words of a simple prayer I learned from my Russian Orthodox father: Creator, Comforter, Spirit of truth, present everywhere, filling all things, treasury of blessings, giver of life, abide in us. Cleanse us from every stain. Save us all, gracious Lord.

4. Merton, "Letters to a White Liberal," in *Seeds of Destruction,* 9.

5. Dear, "Afterword," in Oyer, *Pursuing the Spiritual Roots of Protest,* 233.

6. Merton, *Asian Journal,* 340.

Afterword

As someone who has spent the last seventeen years welcoming guests from all over the world to the Thomas Merton Center, introducing Merton's writings to groups young and old, there has always been the challenge of where to start in his writings. How can you briefly capture the complexity of this contemplative monk and public intellectual? I am not sure I would easily succeed at preparing an elevator speech about Merton unless the building were very tall and the elevator quite slow.

Like Merton, Paul Dekar is a multifaceted person. Paul has influenced a couple of spheres of my life—Merton studies and peace and justice activism through our work with the Fellowship of Reconciliation. His writing and speaking in both areas, connected through Merton's interest in nonviolence and social justice, succeed in weaving together complex threads of Christian tradition and historical justice advocacy into a cohesive body of work accessible and relevant to us today. It is no wonder Paul found in Micah 6:8 an apt encapsulation of the way Merton modeled living out an ancient scriptural tradition in the modern era. Thus, Paul has shown readers of this book not only a way to further their study of Merton's writings, but also a way to live out Merton's method of biblical just action in contemporary times.

Modern readers of sacred scripture and of Merton face some of the same obstacles to doing justice, loving kindness, and walking humbly with God, as were faced by contemporaries of the prophet Micah some 700 years before Christ. Most of the Earth's people still lack an equitable share of the benefits of modern life despite new treatments for illness, labor-saving technologies, and technologies to grow and produce food on a large scale and protect against drought and famine. Micah's call for justice and kindness is left largely unheeded by those of us living in relative global affluence. Yet, this smaller subset of the materially wealthy suffers from what Merton recognized as a spiritual poverty.

No one in Micah's time nor in the time of Jesus could envision the types of distractions the age of computers and mass media would bring, distracting us from our mortality and dependence on God and distancing us from community. (Even such technologies as social media, which purport to bring people together, have served to further parse people into groups that think alike and alienate us from other groups.) As Paul puts it in chapter 1, "Merton recognized that our devices had become like angels—or the devil—something in the realm of another realm, heaven or hell that had come to stand between them and the real world in which we live." Merton, living at a time now considered a primitive media age compared to our contemporary situation, already recognized the challenges ahead and threat to living in connection with God. Again, as Merton makes a bridge across millennia, connecting the twentieth-century person with a wisdom of ancient times, Paul has bridged the gulf of more than a half century since Merton's writings in the 1940s, 50s, and 60s.

As mentioned, modern communication technologies like social media have sometimes brought together like-thinking people into echo chambers accelerating polarization. Beyond Merton's critique of technology, it is also important to note how Merton promoted reconciliation. Paul uses great examples of how Merton not only did his homework in reading from authors of color on racism and from the best sources of other religious traditions, Merton then struck up intentional friendships which helped him learn about the struggles and differences of diverse people firsthand.

As a starting point on the road to understanding others, Merton believed in self-examination and taking the position of a "guilty bystander" to take a concept from his writings. He writes, "Instead of hating the people you think are war-makers, hate the appetites and disorder in your own soul, which are the causes of war. If you love peace, then hate injustice, hate tyranny, hate greed—but hate these things *in yourself*, not in another."[1] From another writer, this could be misconstrued as an attempt to make everything personal or individual. Though Merton is challenging a person to "walk humbly" and admit personal complicity, the next step is to engage with others and oppose systems which perpetuate oppression and division. Seeing the connection between the personal and political, our own values realized in community, Merton challenges us always to find the "hidden wholeness." This is an integrative vision of humans in relation to nature and to God which Merton describes in his poem "Hagia Sophia." As Paul shows us in his chapter on Ishi, Merton's interest in native peoples demonstrated this holistic outlook. On one hand, Merton wanted

1. Merton, *New Seeds of Contemplation*, 122.

his readers to understand the injustices which had been committed and continue to be committed against indigenous peoples. At the same time, he warned that we have ignored a lesson of interconnection to our own peril. Paul writes that this lesson of interconnection teaches "whatever we do to the Earth, we do to ourselves."

What are we to do now that this wisdom (biblical wisdom and wisdom from other religions and cultures) has been carried into the modern age by Merton, and that Merton has been brought into the twenty-first century by Paul? As Paul has shown, Merton would ask us first to cultivate a connection to God through silent reflection and prayer. We do our homework. Merton's range of interests in other cultures and religions can challenge us to broaden our horizons. Delving deeper into Merton, each chapter of Paul's book becomes a launching point for any of the topics he covers in Merton. Of course, we stay rooted in Scripture. Admitting our complicity of current systems of division or oppression, we reach out to community (and a new community built of people who do not look like us or worship like us or at all). We listen first and engage in dialogue. We act to bring change to unjust systems. We return to prayer. Repeat.

The selected stories Paul recounts in this book are a testament to the way he has lived the ideals and spiritual path Merton described. This is inspiring but maybe intimidating to those of us who would do likewise. Drawing upon one of Paul's many stories in peacebuilding, I will adapt to a different context the words a civil rights veteran told him in 1964: having read this book, you've "crossed a river . . . there's a mountain ahead." Thank you, Paul Dekar, for your help in this dual primer in living biblical justice and understanding Merton.

—Mark C. Meade

Associate Director, Thomas Merton Center,
Bellarmine University.

Bibliography

Achtemeier, E. R. "Righteousness in the OT." In *The Interpreter's Dictionary of the Bible, Vol. 4: R–Z*, edited by George Arthur Buttrich, 80–91. New York: Abingdon, 1962.

Achtemeier, P. J. "Righteousness in the NT." In *The Interpreter's Dictionary of the Bible, Vol. 4: R–Z*, edited by George Arthur Buttrich, 91–99. New York: Abingdon, 1962.

Ackroyd, P. R., and C. F. Evans, eds. *The Cambridge History of the Bible*. Vol. 1, *From the Beginnings to Jerome*. Cambridge: Cambridge University Press, 1970.

Advices and Queries. London: Religious Society of Friends, 1964.

AlexandriaDiocese. "Fr August Thompson Video." *YouTube*, February 22, 2018. https://www.youtube.com/watch?v=VZx3jNOEzms.

Alinsky, Saul D. *Rules for Radicals: A Practical Primer for Realistic Radicals*. New York: Vintage, 1972.

American Friends Service Committee. *Speak Truth to Power: A Quaker Search for an Alternative to Violence*. Philadelphia: American Friends Service Committee, 1955.

The Ante-Nicene Fathers. Edited by Alexander Roberts and James Donaldson. 10 vols. Buffalo, NY: Christian Literature, 1885–87.

Apel, William. "Crisis of Faith: Thomas Merton and the Death of Martin Luther King, Jr." *The Merton Annual* 31 (2018) 67–74.

Aprile, Dianne. *The Abbey of Gethsemani: Place of Peace and Paradox: 150 Years in the Life of America's Oldest Trappist Monastery*. Louisville: Trout Lily, 1998.

Atkinson, Morgan, dir. *The Many Storeys and Last Days of Thomas Merton*. N.p.: Duckworks, Inc., 2015.

———. *Soul Searching: The Journey of Thomas Merton*. N.p.: Duckworks, Inc., 2007.

———. *Uncommon Vision: The Life and Times of John Howard Griffin*. N.p.: Duckworks, Inc., 2011.

Attenborough, Richard, dir. *Gandhi*. Culver City, CA: Columbia Pictures, 1982.

Attwater, Donald. *Dictionary of Saints*. Harmondsworth, UK: Penguin, 1965.

Aubert, Roger. *The Church in a Secularised Society*. Christian Centuries 5. New York: Paulist, 1978.

Bailey, Jim. *The End of Healing: A Novel*. Memphis: Healthy City, 2015.

Baldwin, James. *The Fire Next Time*. 1963. Reprint, New York: Vintage, 1993.

Baldwin, Lewis V., and Paul R. Dekar, eds. *"In an Inescapable Network of Mutuality": Martin Luther King Jr. and the Globalization of an Ethical Ideal*. Eugene, OR: Cascade, 2013.

Beifuss, Joan Turner. *At the River I Stand: Memphis, the 1968 Strike, and Martin Luther King*. Memphis: St. Luke's, 1985.

Berger, Rose Marie. "What Pope Francis Can Teach the US Catholic Church about Thomas Merton (Commentary)." *Religion News*, September 25, 2015. https://religionnews.com/2015/09/25/pope-francis-can-teach-us-catholic-church-thomas-merton-commentary/.

Bettenson, Henry, ed. *Documents of the Christian Church*. Oxford: University Press, 1974.

"Bishop Charles Pasquale Greco." http://www.catholic-hierarchy.org/bishop/bgreco.html.

Bochen, Christine M. "Bread in the Wilderness." In *The Thomas Merton Encyclopedia*, edited by William H. Shannon et al., 30–32. Maryknoll, NY: Orbis, 2002.

———. "Mercy within Mercy within Mercy." Presidential Address, ITMS Seventh General Meeting, June 7, 2001. http://merton.org/ITMS/Seasonal/2001PresidentialAddress.pdf.

———. Rev. of *From the Monastery to the World: The Letters of Thomas Merton and Ernesto Cardenal*, translated and edited by Jessie Sandoval. *Merton Annual* 31 (2018) 204–13.

———. "Sanctity." In *The Thomas Merton Encyclopedia*, edited by William H. Shannon et al., 399–401. Maryknoll, NY: Orbis, 2002.

Brennan, Mike. "Walking with Thomas Merton." In *We Are Already One: Thomas Merton's Message of Hope; Reflections to Honor His Centenary (1915–2015)*, edited by Gray Henry and Jonathan Montaldo, 321–22. Louisville: Fons Vitae, 2014.

Brock, Rita Nakashima, and Rebecca Ann Parker. *Saving Paradise: How Christianity Traded Love of This World for Crucifixion and Empire*. Boston: Beacon, 2008.

Brown, Peter. "The Rise and Function of the Holy Man in Late Antiquity." *Journal of Roman Studies* 61 (1971) 80–101.

———. *The World of Late Antiquity AD 150–750*. New York: Harcourt Brace Jovanovich, 1971.

Brown, Robert McAfee. "The Significance of Puebla for the Protestant Churches in North America." In *Puebla and Beyond: Documents and Commentary*, edited by John Eagleson and Philip Scharper, translated by John Drury, 330–46. Maryknoll, NY: Orbis, 1979.

Buber, Martin. *I and Thou*. Translated by Walter Kaufmann. New York: Scribner's, 1970.

Burdick, Eugene, and William J. Lederer. *The Ugly American*. New York: Fawcett Crest, 1958.

Burridge, Kenelm. *Mambu: A Study of Melanesian Cargo Movements and Their Social and Ideological Background*. New York: Harper & Row, 1960.

———. "Merton, Cargo Cults and *The Geography of Lograire*." *The Merton Annual* 17 (2004) 206–15.

Burton, Patricia A. "Analysis of Thirteen Conferences of the International Thomas Merton Society 1-1989 to 13-2013." http://merton.org/Research/Resources/ITMS-Conference-Analysis.pdf.

Cadorette, Curt, et al., eds. *Liberation Theology: An Introductory Reader*. Maryknoll, NY: Orbis, 1992.

Cai, Weiyi, and Simone Landon. "Attacks by White Extremists Are Growing. So Are Their Connections." *New York Times*, April 3, 2019. https://www.nytimes.com/interactive/2019/04/03/world/white-extremist-terrorism-christchurch.

html?mtrref=www.google.com&gwh=D0190EAF7D0E6FDFF3B61F329A903D3
9&gwt=regi&assetType=REGIWALL.

Calvin, John. *Institutes of the Christian Religion*. Edited by John T. McNeill. Translated by Ford Lewis Battles. 2 vols. Philadelphia: Westminster, 1960.

Campbell, Kate. "Prayer of Thomas Merton." Written by Thomas Merton and Kate Campbell. On *For the Living of These Days*. Large River Music, 2006.

———. "They Killed Him." Written by Kris Kristofferson. On *For the Living of These Days*. Large River Music, 2006.

Cardenal, Ernesto. *The Gospel in Solentiname*. Translated by Donald D. Walsh. Maryknoll, NY: Orbis, 1982.

———. "Nicaragua: The Challenge of Revolution." In *The Church in Latin America, 1492–1992*, edited by Enrique Dussel, 265–70. Maryknoll, NY: Orbis, 1992.

Carnes, Jim. *Us and Them: A History of Intolerance in America*. Oxford: Oxford University Press, 1994.

Carson, Clayborne, and Kris Shepard, eds. *A Call to Conscience: The Landmark Speeches of Dr. Martin Luther King, Jr*. New York: Time Warner Audio Books, 2001.

Chadwick, Owen, ed. and trans. *Western Asceticism*. Library of Christian Classics 12. Philadelphia: Westminster, 1958.

Charters, Ann, ed. *The Portable Sixties Reader*. New York: Penguin, 2003.

Cienski, Jan. "Remains of Last Member of California Tribe Go Home at Last." *National Post*, August 9, 2000.

Cleaver, Eldridge. *Soul on Ice*. New York: Delta, 1968.

Cloutier, David. "Beyond Just War: Pope Francis and Just Peace." *Catholic Moral Theology* (blog), June 3, 2014. https://catholicmoraltheology.com/beyond-just-war-pope-francis-and-justpeace/.

Cobb, James C. *The Most Southern Place on Earth: The Mississippi Delta and the Roots of Regional Identity*. Oxford: Oxford University Press, 1992.

Cornell, Tom. Review of *Thomas Merton on Peace*, edited by Gordon C. Zahn. *Fellowship* 40 (1974) 23.

Cuadra, Pablo Antonio. *The Jaguar and the Moon*. Translated by Thomas Merton. Greensboro, NC: Unicorn, 1974.

Cunningham, Lawrence S. *Thomas Merton and the Monastic Vision*. Grand Rapids: Eerdmans, 1999.

Daggy, Robert E., ed. *The Road to Joy: The Letters of Thomas Merton to New and Old Friends*. New York: Farrar, Straus & Giroux, 1989.

Day, Dorothy. "Foreword." In *Ishi Means Man: Essays on Native Americans.*, by Thomas Merton, vii–viii. 1967. Reprint, New York: Paulist, 2015.

de Bary, Wm. Theodore, Wing-tsit Chan, and Burton Watson, compilers. *Sources of Chinese Tradition*. 2 vols. New York: Columbia University Press, 1964.

Deignan, Kathleen. "Children of the Resurrection: Thomas Merton and the Shakers." In *We Are Already One*, edited by Gray Henry and Jonathan Montaldo, 181–86. Louisville: Fons Vitae, 2015.

Dekar, Paul R. "Baptist Friendship Tour to Nicaragua." *Peace Work* #6 (May-August 1986) 6.

———. "Christians, Jews and the Holy Land." *Canadian Society of Church History Papers* (1984) 117–39.

———. *Community of the Transfiguration: The Journey of a New Monastic Community*. Eugene, OR: Cascade, 2008.

———. "Compassion: Central America's Only Hope." *World Vision Actions* (1986).

———. *Creating the Beloved Community: A Journey with the Fellowship of Reconciliation.* Telford, PA: Cascadia, 2005.

———. *Dangerous People: The Fellowship of Reconciliation Building a Nonviolent World of Justice, Peace, and Freedom.* Virginia Beach, VA: Donning, 2016.

———. "Divinization in Merton." Paper read at the 13th ITMS General Meeting, Bridgeport, Connecticut, June 2013.

———. "Does the State of Israel Have Theological Significance?" *Conrad Grebel Review* 2 (1984) 31–46.

———. *For the Healing of the Nations: Baptist Peacemakers.* Macon, GA: Smyth and Helwys, 1993.

———. "Gandhi, Satyagraha, and the Israel-Palestine Conflict." *Acorn: Journal of the Gandhi-King Society* (2007) 21–30.

———. "God's Messenger: Thomas Merton's Embrace of 'the Other' as Reflected in Letters with Ernesto Cardenal." Proposal, 18th ITMS General Meeting, Notre Dame, Indiana, 2021.

———. "God's Messenger: Thomas Merton on Racial Justice." *The Merton Annual* 32 (2019) 137–54.

———. "Hero or Villain? Columbus Began Earth's Destruction." *Canadian Baptist* (July-August 1992) 27, 29–30.

———. *Holy Boldness: Practices of an Evangelistic Lifestyle.* Macon, GA: Smyth & Helwys, 2004.

———. "'I *Am* a Man': Somebodyness and the Dignity of Labor in Dr. King's Last Campaign." *Memphis Theological Seminary Journal* 44 (2008) 59–69.

———. "Ishi: Messenger of Hope." In *We Are Already One: Thomas Merton's Message of Hope; Reflections to Honor His Centenary (1915–2015),* edited by Gray Henry and Jonathan Montaldo, 232–34. Louisville: Fons Vitae, 2014.

———. "Martin Luther King Jr. and Nonviolent Justice Seekers in Latin America and the Caribbean." In *Nonviolence for the 3rd Millennium,* edited by G. Simon Harak, 137–54. Macon, GA: Mercer University Press, 2000.

———. "Peacemaking in Central America." *Atlantic Baptist* 22 (1968) 38–41.

———. "The Peace Movement in Israel." *Conflict Quarterly* 5 (1985) 53–66.

———. "The Power of Silence." *Fellowship* 69 (2003) 15–16.

———. Review of *Interreligious Dialogue: An Anthology of Voices Bridging Cultural and Religious Divides,* edited by Christoffer H. Grundmann. *Missiology* 46.4 (2018) 430–31.

———. Review of *The Martyrdom of Thomas Merton: An Investigation,* by Hugh Turley and David Martin. *The Merton Seasonal* 43.4 (2018) 37–39.

———. Review of *A Poor and Merciful Church: The Illuminative Ecclesiology of Pope Francis,* by Stan Chu Ilo. *Missiology,* forthcoming.

———. Review of *Returning to Reality: Thomas Merton's Wisdom for a Technological World,* by Phillip M. Thompson. *The Merton Seasonal* 38.1 (2013) 39–40.

———. Review of *Signs of Peace: The Interfaith Letters of Thomas Merton,* edited William Apel. *The Merton Annual* 20 (2007) 344–46.

———. Review of *Superabundantly Alive: Thomas Merton's Dance with the Feminine,* by Susan McCaslin and J. S. Porter. *Hamilton Arts and Literature,* December 17, 2018.

———. Review of *Thomas Merton: Cold War Letters,* edited by Christine M. Bochen and William H. Shannon. *Crosscurrents* 51 (2009) 92–93.

————. Review Symposium of *Pursuing the Spiritual Roots of Protest: Merton, Berrigan, Yoder, and Muste at the Gethsemani Abbey Peacemakers Retreat*, by Gordon Oyer. *The Merton Annual* 28 (2015) 224–28.

————. "Silence as Attention and Antidote." *The Merton Seasonal* 40.1 (2015) 16–18.

————. "Swadeshi in Colombia." In *The 17th Annual Gandhi Peace Festival*, 14–15. A publication of the 17th Annual Gandhi Peace Festival, Centre for Peace Studies, McMaster University, Hamilton, Ontario, October 3, 2009.

————. "Thich Nhat Hanh, Martin Luther King, Jr. and Thomas Merton on Retreat." *Weavings* 30 (2014) 10–15.

————. "Thomas Merton, Gandhi, the 'Uprising' of Youth in the '60s, and Building Non-violent Movements Today." *The Merton Seasonal* 31.4 (2006) 16–23.

————. "Thomas Merton on Gandhi." In *Merton and Hinduism*, edited by David Odorisio. Louisville: Fons Vitae, forthcoming.

————. "Thomas Merton on Gandhi and Nonviolence." In *Living Gandhi Today*, 12–14. A publication of the 18th Annual Gandhi Peace Festival, Centre for Peace Studies, McMaster University, Hamilton, Ontario, October 2, 2010.

————. *Thomas Merton: Twentieth-Century Wisdom for Twenty-First-Century Living.* Eugene, OR: Cascade, 2011.

Delhaye, Philippe. "Pope John Paul II on the Contemporary Importance of St. Irenaeus." *L'Osservatore Romano*, English edition, February 9, 1967, 6.

Doherty, Catherine de Hueck. *Poustinia: Christian Spirituality of the East for Western Man.* Notre Dame: Ave Maria, 1975.

————. *Essential Writings.* Selected with an introduction by David Merconi. Maryknoll, NY: Orbis, 2009.

————. *Fragments of My Life.* Notre Dame: Ave Maria, 1979.

Douglass, James W. *Gandhi and the Unspeakable: His Final Experiment with Truth.* Maryknoll, NY: Orbis, 2012.

Douglass, Shelley M. "A Life of Integrity." In *Nonviolence for the Third Millennium*, edited by G. Simon Harak, 155–65. Macon, GA: Mercer University Press, 2000.

————. Review of *Merton & Indigenous Wisdom*, edited by Peter Savastano. *The Merton Seasonal* 45.1 (2020) 34–36.

Dozier, Verna J. *The Dream of God: A Call to Return.* Cambridge: Cowley, 1991.

Dussel, Enrique D. "Theology of Liberation and Marxism." In *Mysterium Liberationis: Fundamental Concepts of Liberation Theology*, edited by Ignacio Ellacuría and Jon Sobrino, 85–102. Maryknoll, NY: Orbis, 1993.

Dussel, Enrique, ed. *The Church in Latin America, 1492–1992.* Maryknoll, NY: Orbis, 1992.

Eckert, Nora. "Tennessee Governor Faces Backlash for Honoring Confederate General and KKK Leader." *NPR*, July 14, 2019. https://www.npr.org/2019/07/14/741629271/tennessee-governor-faces-backlash-for-honoring-confederate-general-and-kkk-leade.

Ellacuría, Ignacio, and Jon Sobrino, eds. *Mysterium Liberationis: Fundamental Concepts of Liberation Theology.* Maryknoll, NY: Orbis, 1993.

Erickson, Lori. "Thomas Merton's Mystical Vision in Louisville." *Spiritual Travels* (blog), n.d. https://www.spiritualtravels.info/spiritual-sites-around-the-world/north-america/kentucky-a-thomas-merton-tour/thomas-mertons-mystical-vision-in-louisville/.

Ferlinghetti, Lawrence. *A Coney Island of the Mind.* New York: New Directions, 1958.

Finlan, Stephen, and Vladimir Kharlamov, eds. *Theōsis: Deification in Christian Theology.* Eugene, OR: Pickwick, 2006.

Fischer, Louis. *The Life of Mahatma Gandhi.* New York: Harper & Row, 1950.

"The Forest Is My Bride." https://www.scholaministries.org/lectory/the-forest-is-my-bride-thomas-mertons-writings-on-nature/.

Forest, James H. "The Gift of Merton." https://jimandnancyforest.com/2011/09/gift-of-merton.

Forest, Jim. *Living with Wisdom: A Life of Thomas Merton.* Maryknoll, NY: Orbis, 2008.

———. Introduction to Thomas Merton's "Application for Conscientious Objector Status—March 1941." *The Merton Annual* 28 (2015) 24–29.

Francis, Pope. "Address of the Holy Father." Visit to the Joint Session of the United States Congress, Washington, DC, September 24, 2015. *Merton Annual* 28 (2015): 16–23.

Friessen, John. "Parliament of the World's Religions Conference Promotes Peace amidst Religious Tensions." *Toronto Globe and Mail,* November 5, 2018.

Galeano, Eduardo. *Memory of Fire.* Vol. 3, *Century of the Wind.* Translated by Cedric Belfrage. New York: Norton, 1998.

Gandhi, Mahatma. *All Men Are Brothers: Life and Thoughts of Mahatma Gandhi as Told in His Own Words.* Paris: UNESCO, 1958.

———. *An Autobiography: The Story of My Experiments with Truth.* Boston: Beacon, 1957.

———. *Gandhi on Non-Violence: Selected Texts from Mohandas K. Gandhi's "Non-violence in Peace and War."* Edited by Thomas Merton. New York: New Directions, 1965.

———. "Mahatma Gandhi Lectures on Nonviolence." https://www.humanities.mcmaster.ca/gandhi/lectures/index.html.

Golemboski, David. "Mysterious, Unaccountable Mixture of Good and Evil." *The Merton Annual* 30 (2017) 88–101.

Gomes, Robin. "Pope Lifts Suspension on Nicaraguan Priest Fr. Ernesto Cardenal." *Vatican News,* February 19, 2019. https://www.vaticannews.va/en/pope/news/2019-02/pope-francis-lifts-sanctions-ernesto-cardenal.html.

Griffin, John Howard. *Black Like Me.* New York: New American Library, 1961.

———. *Follow the Ecstasy: Thomas Merton, the Hermitage Years, 1965–1968.* Fort Worth, TX: Latitudes, 1983.

Grip, Bob. "Henri Nouwen on Thomas Merton." *YouTube,* January 23, 2019. https://www.youtube.com/watch?v=dJoZUF7sbZo.

Habel, Norman, ed. *Readings from the Perspective of. Earth.* Cleveland: Pilgrim, 2000.

Handy, Robert T. *A Christian America: Protestant Hopes and Historical Realities.* New York: Oxford University Press, 1971.

Harpur, Tom. *The Pagan Christ. Recovering the Lost Light.* Toronto: Allen, 2004.

Herbert, George. *The Country Parson; The Temple.* Edited by John N. Wall Jr. New York: Paulist, 1981.

Hillis, Gregory K. "Letters to a Black Catholic Priest: Thomas Merton, Fr. August Thompson and the Civil Rights Movement." *The Merton Annual* 32 (2019) 114–36.

———. "A Sign of Contradiction: Fr. August Thompson, 1926–2019." *Commonweal,* August 26, 2019. https://www.commonwealmagazine.org/sign-contradiction.

Hinson, E. Glenn. "'Thomas Merton, My Brother': The Impact of Thomas Merton on My Life and Thought." *The Merton Annual* 11 (1998) 88–96.

Holson, Laura M. "Sainthood of Junípero Serra Reopens Wounds of Colonialism in California." *New York Times,* September 29, 2015.

Houck, Davis W., and David E. Dixon, eds. *Rhetoric, Religion, and the Civil Rights Movement, 1954–1965*. Waco: Baylor University Press, 2006.

Hugo, Victor. "Speech of Victor Hugo to the Peace Congress at Paris." *Sydney Morning Herald*, December 26, 1849. https://trove.nla.gov.au/newspaper/article/12914658.

Ignatius. *The Spiritual Exercises of St. Ignatius*. Translated by Anthony Mottola. Garden City: Image, 1964.

Ingram, William T., Jr., ed. *A History of Memphis Theological Seminary of the Cumberland Presbyterian Church, 1852–1990*. Memphis: Memphis Theological Seminary, 1990.

The Interpreter's Dictionary of the Bible. Edited by George Arthur Buttrick. 5 vols. New York: Abingdon, 1962.

Irenaeus. *Against Heresies*. In *The Ante-Nicene Fathers*, edited by Alexander Roberts and James Donaldson, 1:315–567. Grand Rapids: Eerdmans, 1885.

Katope, Christopher George, and Paul G. Zolbrod. *Beyond Berkeley: A Sourcebook in Student Values*. Cleveland: World Publishing, 1966.

Kazantzakis, Nikos. *Report to Greco*. Translated by P. A. Bien. New York: Simon & Schuster, 1961.

Kelley, William Melvin. *A Different Drummer*. New York: Doubleday, 1962.

Kelty, Matthew. *Singing for the Kingdom: The Last of the Homilies*. Edited by William O. Paulsell. Collegeville, MN: Liturgical, 2008.

Kilcourse, George. *Ace of Freedoms: Thomas Merton's Christ*. Notre Dame: University of Notre Dame Press, 1993.

King, Martin Luther, Jr. *The Autobiography of Martin Luther King, Jr*. Edited by Clayborne Carson. New York: Time Warner, 1998.

———. "Beyond Vietnam." In *A Call to Conscience: The Landmark Speeches of Dr. Martin Luther King, Jr.*, edited by Clayborne Carson and Kris Shepard, 133–64. New York: Time Warner Audio Books, 2001.

———. *A Testament of Hope: The Essential Writings*. Edited by James M. Washington. San Francisco: Harper & Row, 1986.

———. "Thou, Dear God": Prayers That Open Hearts and Spirits*. Edited by Lewis V. Baldwin. Boston: Beacon, 2012.

King, Robert H. *Thomas Merton and Thich Nhat Hanh: Engaged Spirituality in an Age of Globalization*. New York: Continuum, 2001.

Kolbert, Elizabeth. "Human Nature." *The New Yorker*, May 28, 2007.

Kroeber, Theodora. *Ishi in Two Worlds: A Biography of the Last Wild Indians in North America*. Berkeley: University of California Press, 1964.

Labrie, Ross, and Angus Stuart, eds. *Thomas Merton, Monk on the Edge*. North Vancouver: Thomas Merton Society of Canada, 2012.

Lennon, John. "Imagine." Written by John Lennon. On *Imagine*. EMi Records Ltd., 1971.

Levrier-Jones, George. "The Intriguing Lost Conversation of the Civil Rights Movement: The Writer and the Monk—James Baldwin and Thomas Merton." *History is Now Magazine*, June 15, 2015. www.historyisnowmagazine.com/blog/2015/6/15/the-intriguing-lost-conversation-of-the-civil-right-movement-the-writer-and-the-monk-james-baldwin-and-thomas-merton.

Lipsey, Roger. *Make Peace before the Sun Goes Down: The Long Encounter of Thomas Merton and His Abbot, James Fox*. Boulder, CO: Shambhala, 2015.

Lochhead, David. *The Dialogical Imperative: A Christian Reflection on Interfaith Encounter*. Maryknoll, NY: Orbis, 1988.

Lopez, Elias E. "Ernesto Cardenal, Nicaraguan Priest, Poet and Revolutionary, Dies at 95." *New York Times*, March 1, 2020.

Lucas, F. Dean. *Merton's Abbot: The Life and Times of Dom James Fox*. Lexington, KY: Lucas, 2016.

Luther, Martin. *The Catholic Epistles*. Vol. 30 of *Luther's Works*. Edited by Jaroslav Pelikan. Translated by Martin H. Bertram. St. Louis: Concordia, 1967.

Marty, Martin E. "An Interview about Thomas Merton with Dr. Martin E. Marty." *The Merton Annual* 25 (2012) 23–29.

Matthews, Gray. "Sacred Disrupters as Spiritual Guides." Review of *Thomas Merton and Henri Nouwen: Spiritual Guides for the 21st Century* (12 lectures on 4 CDs), by Michael W. Higgins. *The Merton Seasonal* 44.1 (2019) 33–35.

McCaslin, Susan, and J. S. Porter. *Superabundantly Alive: Thomas Merton's Dance with the Feminine*. Vancouver: Wood Lake, 2018.

McGrath, Alister E. *Historical Theology: An Introduction to the History of Christian Thought*. Hoboken: Wiley Blackwell, 2012.

McMillan, Allan M. "Seven Lessons for Inter-faith Dialogue and Thomas Merton." *The Merton Annual* 15 (2002) 194–209.

Meade, Mark C. "The Reality of Personal Relationships Saves Everything." *The Merton Seasonal* 44.3 (2019) 3–5. http://merton.org/ITMS/Seasonal/44/44-3Meade.pdf.

Mendes-Flohr, Paul R, ed. *A Land of Two Peoples: Martin Buber on Jews and Arabs*. Oxford: Oxford University Press, 1983.

Merton, Thomas. *The Asian Journal of Thomas Merton*. Edited by Naomi Burton et al. New York: New Directions, 1973.

———. *The Behavior of Titans*. New York: New Directions, 1961.

———. *Bread in the Wilderness*. New York: New Directions, 1960.

———. *Cassian and the Fathers: Initiation into the Monastic Tradition 1*. Edited by Patrick F. O'Connell. Kalamazoo, MI: Cistercian, 2005.

———. *Cold War Letters*. Edited by Christine M. Bochen and William H. Shannon. Maryknoll, NY: Orbis, 2006.

———. *Compassionate Fire: The Letters of Thomas Merton and Catherine de Hueck Doherty*. Edited by Robert A. Wild. Notre Dame: Ave Maria, 2009.

———. *Conjectures of a Guilty Bystander*. Garden City, NY: Doubleday, 1966.

———. *Contemplation in a World of Action*. Notre Dame: University of Notre Dame Press, 1998.

———. *The Courage for Truth: The Letters of Thomas Merton to Writers*. Selected and edited by Christine M. Bochen. New York: Farrar, Straus and Giroux, 1993.

———. *Dancing in the Water of Life: Seeking Peace in the Hermitage*. Vol. 5 of *The Journals of Thomas Merton, 1963–1965*. Edited by Robert E. Daggy. San Francisco: HarperCollins, 1995.

———. "Day of a Stranger." In *A Thomas Merton Reader*, edited by Thomas P. McDonnell, 431–38. Garden City, NY: Image, 1974.

———. *Dialogues with Silence: Prayers and Drawings*. Edited by Jonathan Montaldo. San Francisco: Harper, 2001.

———. *Elected Silence: The Autobiography of Thomas Merton*. London: Hollis and Carter, 1949.

———. *Entering the Silence: Becoming a Monk and a Writer*. Vol. 2 of *The Journals of Thomas Merton, 1941–1952*. Edited by Jonathan Montaldo. San Francisco: HarperCollins, 1997.

———. *Essential Writings*. Edited by Christine M. Bochen. Maryknoll, NY: Orbis, 2000.

———. *Faith and Violence: Christian Teaching and Christian Practice*. Notre Dame: University of Notre Dame Press, 1968.

———. "Foreword." In *Vietnam: Lotus in a Sea of Fire*, by Thich Nhat Hanh, vii–x. New York: Hill and Wang, 1967.

———. *From the Monastery to the World: The Letters of Thomas Merton and Ernesto Cardenal*. Translated and edited by Jessie Sandoval. Berkeley, CA: Counterpoint, 2017.

———. "Gandhi and the One-Eyed Giant." In *Gandhi on Non-Violence: A Selection from the Writings of Mahatma Gandhi*, by Mahatma Gandhi, edited by Thomas Merton, 1–20. New York: New Directions, 1964.

———. *The Hidden Ground of Love: The Letters of Thomas Merton on Religious Experience and Social Concerns*. Edited by William H. Shannon. New York: Farrar, Straus & Giroux, 1985.

———. *Hidden in the Same Mystery: Thomas Merton and Loretto*. Edited by Bonnie Thurston et al. Louisville: Fons Vitae, 2010.

———. "In the Wilderness." *The Merton Seasonal* 40.2 (2015) 3–7.

———. *An Introduction to Christian Mysticism: Initiation into the Monastic Tradition 3*. Edited by Patrick F. O'Connell. Kalamazoo, MI: Cistercian, 2008.

———. "Introduction." In *The Prison Meditations of Father Alfred Delp*, vii–xxvi. New York: Herder & Herder, 1963.

———. *Ishi Means Man: Essays on Native Americans*. 1967. Reprint, New York: Paulist, 2015.

———. *The Last of the Fathers: Saint Bernard of Clairvaux and the Encyclical Letter, "Doctor Mellifluus."* New York: Harcourt, Brace, 1954.

———. *The Literary Essays of Thomas Merton*. Edited by Patrick Hart. New York: New Directions, 1981.

———. *Loretto and Gethsemani*. [Talk commemorating the 150th anniversary of the founding of the Congregation of The Sisters of Loretto, 1812–1962.] Trappist, KY: Abbey of Gethsemani, 1962.

———. *Love and Living*. Edited by Naomi Burton Stone and Patrick Hart. New York: Farrar, Straus & Giroux, 1979.

———. *The Monastic Journey*. Edited by Patrick Hart. Garden City, NY: Image, 1978.

———. *Monastic Observances: Initiation into the Monastic Tradition 5*. Edited by Patrick F. O'Connell. Kalamazoo, MI: Cistercian, 2010.

———. *Mystics and Zen Masters*. New York: Dell, 1967.

———. *The New Man*. New York: Bantam, 1981.

———. *New Seeds of Contemplation*. New York: New Directions, 1962.

———. *No Man Is an Island*. New York: Harcourt, Brace, 1955.

———. *The Nonviolent Alternative*. Edited by Gordon C. Zahn. New York: Farrar, Straus & Giroux, 1980.

———. *Original Child Bomb: Meditations on the Origin of the Atomic Age*. New York: New Directions, 1962.

———. *The Other Side of the Mountain: The End of the Journey*. Vol. 7 of *The Journals of Thomas Merton, 1967–1968*. Edited by Patrick Hart. San Francisco: HarperCollins, 1998.

———. *Passion for Peace: The Social Essays*. Edited by William H. Shannon. New York: Crossroad, 1997.

———. *Peace in the Post-Christian Era*. Edited by Patricia A. Burton. Maryknoll, NY: Orbis, 2004.

———. *Praying the Psalms*. Collegeville, MN: Liturgical, 1956.

———. *Pre-Benedictine Monasticism: Initiation into the Monastic Tradition 2*. Edited by Patrick F. O'Connell. Kalamazoo, MI: Cistercian, 2006.

———. *Raids on the Unspeakable*. New York: New Directions, 1966.

———. *The Rule of Saint Benedict: Initiation into the Monastic Tradition 4*. Edited by Patrick F. O'Connell. Kalamazoo, MI: Cistercian, 2009.

———. *Run to the Mountain*. Vol. 1 of *The Journals of Thomas Merton, 1939–1941*. Edited by Patrick Hart. San Francisco: HarperCollins, 1996.

———. *The School of Charity: Letters on Religious Renewal and Spiritual Direction*. Edited by Patrick Hart. New York: Farrar, Straus & Giroux, 1990.

———. *A Search for Solitude: Pursuing the Monk's True Life*. Vol. 3 of *The Journals of Thomas Merton, 1952–1960*. Edited by Lawrence S. Cunningham. San Francisco: Harper, 1996.

———. *Seeds of Destruction*. New York: Farrar, Straus & Giroux, 1964.

———. *The Seven Storey Mountain*. New York: Harcourt, Brace, 1948.

———. *Sign of Jonas*. Garden City, NY: Image, 1956.

———. *Signs of Peace: The Interfaith Letters of Thomas Merton*. Edited by William Apel. Maryknoll, NY: Orbis, 2006.

———. *Silence in Heaven: A Book on the Monastic Life*. New York: Crowell, 1956.

———. *The Silent Life*. New York: Farrar, Straus & Cudahy, 1957.

———. "Some Points from the Birmingham Non-violence Movement." *The Merton Annual* 25 (2012) 13–22.

———. *The Springs of Contemplation: A Retreat at the Abbey of Gethsemani*. Edited by Jane Marie Richardson. New York: Farrar, Straus & Giroux, 1992.

———. *Survival or Prophecy? The Letters of Thomas Merton and Jean Leclercq*. Edited by Patrick Hart. New York: Farrar, Straus & Giroux, 2008.

———. *Thomas Merton: A Life in Letters*. Edited by William H. Shannon and Christine M. Bochen. New York: Harper, 2008.

———. *Thomas Merton on Saint Bernard*. Cistercian Studies 9. Kalamazoo, MI: Cistercian, 1980.

———. *A Thomas Merton Reader*. Edited by Thomas McDonnell. Rev. ed. Garden City, NY: Image, 1974.

———. *Thomas Merton, Spiritual Master: The Essential Writings*. Edited by Lawrence S. Cunningham. Mahwah, NJ: Paulist, 1992.

———. *Thoughts in Solitude*. New York: Farrar, Straus & Cudahy, 1958.

———. *Turning toward the World: The Pivotal Years*. Vol. 4 of *The Journals of Thomas Merton, 1960–1963*. Edited by Victor A. Kramer. San Francisco: HarperCollins, 1996.

———. *The Waters of Siloe*. New York: Harcourt, Brace, 1949.

———. *The Way of Chuang Tzu*. New York: New Directions, 1965.

———. *What Is Contemplation?* Notre Dame: Saint Mary's College, 1948.

———. *When the Trees Say Nothing: Writings on Nature*. Edited by Kathleen Deignan. Notre Dame: Sorin, 2003.

———. *Witness to Freedom: Letters in Times of Crisis.* Edited by William H. Shannon. New York: Farrar, Straus & Giroux, 1994.

———. *Words of Peace: Thomas Merton on Nonviolence.* Edited by Gordon Zahn. Erie, PA: Benet, 1989.

———. *Zen and the Birds of Appetite.* New York: New Directions, 1968.

Merton, Thomas, trans. *The Wisdom of the Desert: Sayings from the Desert Fathers of the Fourth Century.* New York: New Directions, 1960.

Metaxas, Eric. *Bonhoeffer: Pastor, Martyr, Prophet, Spy.* Nashville: Nelson, 2011.

Mills, Selena. "What Are Land Acknowledgements and Why Do They Matter?" *Local Love* (blog), March 18, 2019. https://locallove.ca/issues/what-are-land-acknowledgements-and-why-do-they-matter/#.XqmaKW5Fx9M.

Mott, Michael. *The Seven Mountains of Thomas Merton.* London: Sheldon, 1986.

Neufeld, Hugo. *The North End Lives: A Journey through Poverty Terrain.* Scottdale, PA: Herald, 2006.

Neusner, Jacob. "Shalom: Complementarity." In *Ministry and Theology in Global Perspective: Contemporary Challenges for the Church*, edited by Don A. Pittman et al., 465–71. Grand Rapids: Eerdmans, 1996.

Nhat Hanh, Thich. *Anger: Wisdom for Cooling the Flames.* New York: Riverhead, 2001.

———. *Being Peace.* Berkeley, CA: Parallax, 1987.

———. *Essential Writings.* Edited by Robert Ellsberg. Maryknoll, NY: Orbis, 2001.

———. *The Miracle of Being Awake.* Nyack, NY: Fellowship, 1975.

———. *Peace Is Every Step: The Path of Mindfulness in Everyday Life.* New York: Bantam, 1991.

Nicholl, Donald. *Holiness.* London: Darton, Longman & Todd, 1981.

Norris, Kathleen. *The Cloister Walk.* New York: Riverhead, 1996.

Nouwen, Henri J. M. *The Genesee Diary.* Garden City, NY: Doubleday, 1976.

———. *The Return of the Prodigal Son: A Story of Homecoming.* New York: Continuum, 1995.

"Obituary, August Thompson." *ITMS Newsletter* 26.3 (2019) 4–5.

O'Connell, Patrick. "Civil Rights Movement." In *The Thomas Merton Encyclopedia*, edited by William H. Shannon et al., 377–79. Maryknoll, NY: Orbis, 2002.

———. "Editor's Preface." *Merton Seasonal* 40.1 (Spring 2015) 1–2.

———. "Racism." In *The Thomas Merton Encyclopedia*, edited by William H. Shannon et al., 60–62. Maryknoll, NY: Orbis, 2002.

O'Connor, Elizabeth. *Journey Inward, Journey Outward.* New York: Harper & Row, 1968.

O'Hare, Padraic. "Thomas Merton and Educative Dialogue among Diverse Christians." *The Merton Seasonal* 45.1 (2020) 15–22.

Oyer, Gordon. *Pursuing the Spiritual Roots of Protest: Merton, Berrigan, Yoder, and Muste at the Gethsemani Abbey Peacemakers Retreat.* Eugene, OR: Cascade, 2014.

Patterson, Stephen J., et al. *The Fifth Gospel: The Gospel of Thomas Comes of Age.* New York: T. & T. Clark, 2011.

Payton, James R., Jr. *Light from the Christian East: An Introduction to the Orthodox Tradition.* Downers Grove, IL: IVP Academic, 2007.

Pearson, Paul M. "A Voice for Racial Justice." *The Merton Seasonal* 40.1 (2015) 46–47.

Pelikan, Jaroslav. *The Emergence of the Catholic Tradition (100–600).* Vol. 1 of *The Christian Tradition: A History of the Development of Doctrine.* Chicago: University of Chicago Press, 1971.

Penkett, Luke. *Touched by God's Spirit: The Influence of Merton, Van Gogh, Vanier and Rembrandt on the Compassionate Life of Henri Nouwen.* London: Darton, Longman & Todd, 2019.

Quenon, Paul. *In Praise of the Useless Life: A Monk's Memoir.* Notre Dame: Ave Maria, 2018.

———. Review of *Merton's Abbot: The Life and Times of Dom James Fox,* by Lucas F. Dean. *The Merton Annual* 30 (2017) 274–78.

Reynolds, Henry. *Why Weren't We Told? A Personal Search for the Truth about Our History.* Ringwood, Victoria: Viking, 1999.

Rice, Edward. *The Man in the Sycamore Tree: The Good Times and Hard Life of Thomas Merton.* Garden City, NY: Image, 1972.

Richardson, Cyril C., trans. and ed. *Early Christian Fathers.* Philadelphia: Westminster, 1953.

Rilke, Rainer Maria. *Ahead of All Parting: The Selected Poetry and Prose of Rainer Maria Rilke.* Edited and translated by Stephen Mitchell. New York: Modern Library, 1995.

Rohr, Richard. *The Naked Now.* New York: Crossroad, 2009.

———. "The Strength of the Link." https://cac.org/the-strength-of-the-link-2019 -11-20/.

Ruprecht, Louis A., Jr. *An Elemental Life: Mystery and Mercy in the Work of Father Matthew Kelty, OCSO.* Collegeville, MN: Liturgical, 2018.

Said, Edward W. *Orientalism.* New York: Vintage, 1979.

———. *Reflections on Exile and Other Essays.* Cambridge: Harvard University Press, 2000.

Sandburg, Carl. "Prologue." In *The Family of Man,* 1–2. New York: Simon & Schuster, 1955.

Savio, Mario. "The Berkeley Student Rebellion of 1964." In *Beyond Berkeley,* by Christopher George Katope and Paul G. Zolbrod, 83–89. Cleveland: World Publishing, 1966.

———. "Sit-in Address on the Steps of Sproul Hall." Speech delivered December 2, 1964, University of California, Berkeley. https://www.americanrhetoric.com/ speeches/mariosaviosproulhallsitin.htm.

Sehested, Ken. "Humility." *Prayer and Politiks* (blog), n.d. https://www.prayerandpolitiks. org/other-poems/2014/11/10/humility.1192811.

Shannon, William H. "Freedom Songs." In *The Thomas Merton Encyclopedia,* edited by William H. Shannon et al., 167. Maryknoll, NY: Orbis, 2002.

———. "Humility." In *The Thomas Merton Encyclopedia,* edited by William H. Shannon et al., 215–16. Maryknoll, NY: Orbis, 2002.

———. "Naomi Burton Stone." In *The Thomas Merton Encyclopedia,* edited by William H. Shannon et al., 452–53. Maryknoll, NY: Orbis, 2002.

———. "New Man." In *The Thomas Merton Encyclopedia,* edited by William H. Shannon et al., 322–23. Maryknoll, NY: Orbis, 2002.

Shannon, William H., et al., eds. *The Thomas Merton Encyclopedia.* Maryknoll, NY: Orbis, 2002.

Shepard, Mark. *Gandhi Today. A Report on Mahatma Gandhi's Successors.* Arcata, CA: Simple Productions, 1987.

Shimoni, Gideon. *Gandhi, Satyagraha and the Jews: A Formative Factor in India's Policy towards Israel.* Jerusalem: Papers on Peace Problems, 1977.

Sprinkle, Stephen. "Fr. Matthew Kelty, OCSO, Passes Away." https://unfinishedlivesblog.com/2011/02/18/fr-matthew-kelty-ocso-passes-away-out-gay-monk-was-thomas-mertons-confessor/.

Stavropoulos, Christoforos. "Partakers of Divine Nature." In *Eastern Orthodox Theology: A Contemporary Reader*, edited by Daniel B. Clendenin, 183–92. Grand Rapids: Baker, 1995.

St. Norbert College. "'Racism, White Privilege, and Thomas Merton on Transformative Spirituality and Justice.'" *YouTube*, November 7, 2017. https://www.youtube.com/watch?v=OJvSbhsosy8&feature=emb_title.

Suzuki, David, and Peter Knudtson. *Wisdom of the Elders: Sacred Native Stories of Nature*. New York: Bantam, 1992.

Tate, Tim, and Brad Johnson. *The Assassination of Robert F. Kennedy: Crime, Conspiracy and Cover-Up; a New Investigation*. London: Thistle, 2018.

Thompson, August, and John Howard Griffin. "Dialogue." *Ramparts*, December 25, 1963.

Thompson, Phillip M. *Returning to Reality: Thomas Merton's Wisdom for a Technological World*. Eugene, OR: Cascade, 2012.

Thoreau, Henry David. *Walden and Other Writings*. New York: Modern Library, 1950.

Tyler, Anne. *A Spool of Blue Thread*. New York: Knopf, 2015.

U2. "MLK." Written by Adam Clayton et al. On *The Unforgettable Fire*. Universal-Island Records, 1984.

———. "Sunday, Bloody Sunday." Written by Adam Clayton et al. On *Under a Blood Red Sky*. Universal-Island Records, 2008.

Van der Post, Laurens. *The Dark Eye in Africa*. London: Apollo, 1955.

———. *The Lost World of the Kalahari*. New York: Morrow, 1958.

Van Doren, Mark. *Autobiography*. New York: Greenwood, 1968.

Vanier, Jean. *Encountering "the Other."* New York: Paulist, 2005.

Volf, Miroslav. *Exclusion and Embrace: A Theological Exploration of Identity, Otherness, and Reconciliation*. Nashville: Abingdon, 1996.

Vosper, Gretta. *With or Without God: Why the Way We Live Is More Important than What We Believe*. Toronto: HarperCollins, 2008.

Wadlow, René. "Gambia Invokes Genocide Convention against Myanmar." *Peace Magazine*, January–March 2020.

Walters, Kerry, and Robin Jarrell. *Blessed Peacemakers: 365 Extraordinary People Who Changed the World*. Eugene, OR: Cascade, 2013.

Ware, Timothy. *The Orthodox Church*. Harmondsworth, UK: Penguin, 1963.

Warshaw, Stephen. *The Trouble in Berkeley*. Berkeley, CA: Diablo, 1965.

Weis, Monica. *The Environmental Vision of Thomas Merton*. Lexington: University of Kentucky, 2011.

———. Review of *An Elemental Life: Mystery and Mercy in the Work of Father Matthew Kelty, OCSO*, by Louis A. Ruprecht Jr. *The Merton Seasonal* 44.3 (2019) 28–29.

White, Lynn, Jr. "The Historical Roots of Our Ecological Crisis." *Science* 155 (1967) 1203–7.

Wilderness Society. *The Franklin Blockade*. Hobart, Tasmania: Wilderness Society, 1983.

Wilkes, Paul, ed. *Merton, by Those Who Knew Him Best*. San Francisco: Harper & Row, 1984.

Wilson-Hartgrove, Jonathan. *New Monasticism: What It Has to Say to Today's Church.* Grand Rapids: Brazos, 2008.

Winbush, Raymond A., ed. *Should America Pay? Slavery and the Raging Debate on Reparations.* New York: Amistad, 2003.

Wink, Walter. *The Powers That Be: Theology for a New Millennium.* New York: Doubleday, 1998.

Wyschogrod, Edith. *Saints and Postmodernism: Revisioning Moral Philosophy.* Chicago: University of Chicago Press, 1990.

X, Malcolm. *The Autobiography of Malcolm X.* New York: Random House, 1964.